Shade Garden

Shade Garden

Essential know-how and expert advice for gardening success

CONTENTS

Transform your shady yard into a cool retreat for people amid a host of beautiful plants.

UNDERSTANDING SHADE

When temperatures soar during the summer months, a shady yard really comes into its own, providing a cool, tranquil spot where you can enjoy the warmth of the day in comfort. So, while a shady yard can be challenging, celebrating its benefits will help you see the opportunities it offers. Understanding the type of shade you have in your yard, and what is causing it, enables you to choose plants that will thrive in your conditions and may help identify ways to let in more light, too.

CELEBRATING SHADE

Sitting under a tree on a sunny day listening to the birds is one of life's simple pleasures, while walking through a carpet of colorful leaves crunching underfoot in the fall is another. These are just two of the delights you can enjoy in a shady yard. Added benefits are that soils tend not to dry out quickly, reducing the need for watering, and the color of furniture is not bleached by the sun.

COOL CHOICES

We all love a bright, sunny day, but a yard flooded with light for hours on end can be too much of a good thing. A south-facing yard may be unbearable during the summer, with no relief from the unrelenting rays, while those lucky enough to have some cool shade will find the lower temperatures and light levels more welcoming. However, at other times of the year a little warmth may be desirable, so you also need to consider how to achieve that balance. Planting deciduous trees and shrubs that come into leaf in late spring is a good solution, allowing more sunlight in during the fall and winter.

The list of plants that create shade and that thrive in low light conditions is vast, too, so you will never be short of choices for structural and decorative features in your yard.

Leave fallen leaves to provide a protective layer over the soil rather than raking them up.

REDUCING THE WORKLOAD

Shady spaces can be easier to maintain than sunny yards. Evaporation rates are inevitably lower in the shade, and many low-light plants need little or no watering once established. The lack of sun can also reduce the growth of weeds and the rate at which they flower and set seed. In the fall, raking up the foliage that falls from trees may increase the workload, but you can simply leave it on your beds and borders to create a protective mulch over the soil (see p.57) and provide shelter for wildlife during the cold winter months.

A simple bistro table and chairs in the shade of a tree provides the perfect spot for evening drinks.

Foliage plants create a leafy frill around simple reflective tanks in this elegant shady city space.

TOP TIP TREES COOL THE AIR MORE EFFICIENTLY THAN ARTIFICIAL STRUCTURES BY RELEASING WATER VAPOR FROM THEIR FOLIAGE, SO PLACE SEATING BENEATH THEM FOR ADDED COMFORT IN SUMMER.

WHAT IS CAUSING SHADE?

While some shade in a yard is cause for celebration, if your whole plot is dark and gloomy you may wish to let in more light to make it brighter and widen your plant choices. Assessing what is causing the shade can help you make slight alterations that will increase light levels, although you will just have to work with shade from tall permanent structures such as your house or neighboring buildings.

Removing the lower branches of a tree can increase light levels in the morning or evening when the sun is at an angle.

TREES AND SHRUBS

Mature trees with spreading canopies and large shrubs will cause shade, either in your own yard or in neighboring plots. Check where they cast a shadow at different times of the day; this will be determined by the direction your yard faces (see p.22) and the position of the tree or shrub. If the sun passes behind a tree for many hours each day, it will also create a long shadow during that time, so you will need to choose plants carefully for these darker areas.

Even if a tree is casting more shade than is ideal, aim to retain it if possible, since it will help reduce air pollution while also providing a cool area for seating and possibly increasing the privacy in your yard. To allow more light in, you could ask a tree surgeon or arborist to prune it back, though it may return to its original size within a few years. Alternatively, raise the crown by removing the lower limbs (see pp.28–29). This can sometimes allow low morning and evening light to penetrate, creating sunspots for relaxing or dining when the rays are not too strong.

Trees with airy canopies such as birches create dappled shade that many plants will tolerate.

PERMANENT BUILDINGS

Neighboring properties and your own home may be creating shade in your yard. While there is little you can do about this, you could paint the walls of your house a pale color to reflect more light into the space, and use the shade from it and other buildings to create a seating area. Alternatively, use these darker areas for a shed, sculpture, or fernery (see pp.110–111).

Painting your house a pale color will help reflect sun into the yard and on plants that will benefit from the light.

Tuck a shed into a leafy corner close to trees where it will cast no additional shade over the yard.

GARDEN STRUCTURES

Sheds and storage units that cast shade are often sited at the back of the yard, but this may be the worst place for them if your yard is north-facing and that area receives the most sun. Consider moving them to spots that are in deep shade already, where few plants will thrive and it is too cold to sit, and use the sunnier areas for a flower border or seating and dining areas. The same rule applies if you are thinking of installing a summerhouse or garden room; check how much shade the structure will create and where before making the decision about its location. Bear in mind that a room in shade will be cooler in summer, when these buildings can become unbearably hot.

BOUNDARY DECISIONS

A solid wall that casts dense shade would be costly to replace, but you could have some of it removed to reduce the height. If your fences are creating too much shade, think about replacing them with lower structures; affix trellis panels on top if you want a taller boundary that offers a degree of privacy without robbing you of light. Also consider semitransparent barriers such as picket fencing, woven hurdles, slatted panels, or even a chain link fence, except for areas near seating where you may want some privacy. These screens will allow more light to reach your plants.

Where privacy is not needed, try an open-weave or picket fence to allow more light through.

TYPES OF SHADE

The various obstacles that block sunlight from falling on an area can cast different levels of shade, which will affect both the ambience of the space and the types of plants that you will be able to grow there successfully. The angle, location, and intensity of the sun changes dramatically throughout the year, too, and areas beneath deciduous trees and shrubs may offer the perfect light conditions for plant growth before the leaves unfurl and throw them into deep shade. The terms used in this book refer to the different types of shade that you may find in your yard.

Sunlight falls on some areas of this largely shady space just long enough to sustain a few sun-loving plants.

LIGHT LEVELS EXPLAINED

The terms opposite are used to describe different light levels, while the icons are used throughout this book so you can see at a glance what each plant needs.

You will find the icons on plant labels, too, and there may be more than one where plants tolerate a range of conditions.

In addition to the shade that is caused by plants, walls, and fences, an area of the yard shaded by a temporary artificial screen such as a parasol or awning will also experience low light conditions, so remember to take this into account if you use one for any length of time and you wish to grow plants beneath it.

Flowers such as Japanese anemones thrive in sites that receive three to six hours of direct sun per day.

Flowers such as California poppies prefer a bright area in direct sun.

FULL SUN ☼

The term "full sun" refers to an area that receives six hours or more of direct sunlight each day in midsummer. The same site may receive slightly more or less sun at other times of the year, so check before making final plant choices.

TOP TIP LIGHT LEVELS VARY ENORMOUSLY THROUGHOUT THE YEAR, AND AREAS THAT MAY SEE NO SUN IN THE DEPTHS OF WINTER COULD BE ILLUMINATED FOR MANY HOURS WHEN SUMMER ARRIVES. FOR THIS REASON, IT IS IMPORTANT TO CHECK LIGHT LEVELS IN YOUR YARD DURING DIFFERENT SEASONS (*SEE P.22*).

An area that is open to the sky close to, but not under, a tree may be in light shade.

LIGHT SHADE ☼

This type of shade is usually found in an open site that is exposed to the sky directly above it, but an obstacle such as a fence, wall, or tree casts shade for just a few hours over the space in the height of summer.

Spaces that receive up to six hours of sun in summer are in part shade.

PART SHADE ☼

There is little difference between this term and light shade and they may sometimes be used interchangeably. Part shade refers to an area that receives three to six hours of direct sunlight per day in midsummer. However, the level of light during that time can differ, since midday sun emits more light than morning or evening sun, and this may affect plant growth accordingly.

Dappled shade can be found under a tree before the leaves fully unfurl.

DAPPLED SHADE ☼

The variable light filtering through an open tree canopy or a perforated screen will cast dappled shade. This type of light creates a beautiful ambience in a space and offers protection from strong midday sun at the height of summer.

Trees that allow sun through for two or three hours per day cast moderate shade.

MODERATE SHADE ☼

An area where direct sunlight falls for two or three hours each day in midsummer is said to be in moderate shade. However, as for part shade, light levels will be stronger if those hours are at midday, which may allow a greater number of plants to thrive there.

The areas directly under the tree canopies in this garden are in deep shade.

FULL OR DEEP SHADE ☼

Sites that receive direct sunlight for less than two hours each day in summer are in full or deep shade. Examples include areas beneath evergreen trees or deciduous trees with dense canopies. Buildings, walls, and close-board fences can also create areas of full shade.

HOW SHADE AFFECTS PLANTS

All terrestrial plants need sunlight, carbon dioxide, and water to photosynthesize, the process by which they make the sugars that provide them with energy to grow and reproduce. Some demand high levels of sunlight, others prefer cool shade, while a large number grow happily in a site that's shaded for a few hours each day. Problems occur when sun-lovers are planted in shade and vice versa, but these issues can be avoided by matching the needs of your plants with the light levels in your yard.

Sun-lovers such as *Stachys byzantina* have small, furry, silver leaves that protect them from strong rays.

SUN- VS SHADE-LOVERS

Plants have adapted to thrive in almost every environment on Earth. The species that have evolved to tolerate high levels of sunlight tend to have small, fleshy, pale, or silver leaves that help deflect strong rays and conserve water in hot climates where evaporation rates are high. Many also have hairs on their foliage that protect them from heat stress and trap dew and raindrops.

Plants that are adapted to shade require a larger surface area in order to absorb as much sunlight as possible. Their foliage tends to be dark green with a large surface area, and each leaf contains high levels of chlorophyll, the pigment responsible for absorbing light during photosynthesis.

PLANTS' REACTIONS TO SHADE

If you have sown seeds on a windowsill, you will have noticed that the seedlings stretch toward the light source, and the stems may also grow tall and thin (etiolated) in an effort to reach it. Plants' ability to grow toward the light is known as phototropism, and when sun-loving species are planted in shade, just like the seedlings, they will stretch toward the sun and become misshapen. Those with red, yellow, or silver leaves may lose their color, while flowering will be reduced or may stop altogether where light levels are too low. Plants can eventually die when deprived of the sun they need.

Conversely, shade-loving plants have a reduced phototrophic response and tend not to stretch toward the light. They also grow more slowly and their flowers are often paler in color, an adaptation that makes them more visible to pollinators such as butterflies and bees. Some also use scent to attract insects to their blooms. When these plants are grown in sun, their leaves often become scorched by the strong rays and the damage reduces their ability to photosynthesize, which may cause them to die.

To prevent these symptoms, simply match your plants to the light levels in your yard, and help them thrive by checking that your soil conditions and climate suit their needs (see pp.24–25).

Seedlings will grow tall and thin on a windowsill as they stretch toward the light, a process known as phototropism.

The large, thin leaves of hostas are perfectly adapted to low light and do not have a strong phototropic response.

Many shade-loving plants have large, thin leaves and small, pale flowers that sing out from the gloom.

SHADY INSPIRATIONS

Whether you want to add shade-making plants and features to a sunny yard, have a small urban plot surrounded by tall buildings that needs brightening up, or wish to plant a small copse of trees to evoke a woodland edge, you may need a little inspiration to help you create the look. Browse the ideas here and throughout the book for planting and design tips, and visit public and private gardens to see how others use shady spaces.

Multi-stemmed oaks create the dappled shade loved by blue scillas, euphorbias, aquilegias, and other woodland plants.

LIVEN UP A GLOOMY CORNER

Brighten up a shady corner where few plants thrive with a pot of colorful begonias, which bloom throughout the summer when given just a few hours of sun each day. In darker areas of the yard, consider making a fernery, filling it with a variety of these pretty textural plants, some of which can tolerate very low light levels (*see pp.110–115*).

The red flowers of *Begonia* 'Armour' in this large container sparkle like fireworks in a shady area.

RECREATE A WOODLAND EDGE

The dappled shade beneath mature trees offers many shade-loving plants the perfect niche to establish and thrive. Create a tapestry of flowers and foliage with spring bulbs such as daffodils and scillas and the frothy flowers of euphorbias leading the way in spring, with sedges (*Carex*), geraniums, and blue lily turf (*Liriope*) taking the stage in summer and fall. You could also dress up a mature tree by planting a rambling rose or clematis that will thread through the branches to add another layer of seasonal interest.

MAKE A COOL DINING AREA

Dining under a blazing sun is no fun. You could install a large umbrella to solve the problem, but a vine-covered pergola creates a beautiful natural effect, providing dappled shade during the summer and allowing more light onto your terrace earlier in the year before the leaves unfurl, when the sun's rays are not as strong. A vine may also provide you with a crop of grapes after a warm summer. Other climbers that would cover a large pergola include *Clematis montana*, *Akebia quinata*, and *Parthenocissus henryana*.

A large vine-covered pergola protects a dining area on a patio from hot summer rays.

PLANT A VEGGIE PATCH

Many edible crops like full sun, but a few are tolerant of some shade. Leafy cabbages and lettuces often prefer a bed out of strong midday sun, which will help prevent the latter from running to seed too quickly.

A few herbs will also grow well in part shade and make good bedfellows for the salad leaves. Try cilantro, chives, and parsley in these cooler spots. Mint also enjoys a little shade, but is best confined to a pot of its own where it won't swamp everything in its path within a year or two. For more ideas on growing edibles in shady spaces, see pp.122–127.

A variety of leafy crops will thrive in a small vegetable patch in dappled or part shade that receives a few hours of sun.

Allow a mixture of pollen-rich wild and ornamental plants to jostle for space in a shady corner.

INCLUDE A HOME FOR WILDLIFE

A gloomy area beside a wall or fence will provide the perfect home for many forms of wildlife. Frogs and toads love damp, shady conditions, which are also loved by the slugs and snails they like to eat. Include some pollen-rich flowers such as geraniums and bugle (*Ajuga*), and allow a few weeds to take root if they are not too invasive—dandelions, for example, support a host of bees, butterflies, and day-flying moths and will not overwhelm a densely planted area.

Astrantias thrive in part shade and make perfect partners for many other summer-flowering perennials.

FOCUS ON FLOWERS

Dispel the myth that shady yards are not colorful by planting a range of flowers that thrive in areas of dappled or part shade. Choose from the many perennial plants that enjoy these conditions (*see pp.66–73*), and supplement them with flowering shrubs such as hydrangeas, mahonias, and Mexican orange blossom (*Choisya*) to create a floriferous feast for the eyes.

MAKE EVERY SEASON A WINNER

Remember to consider plants for all seasons when planning your landscaping. Even winter can be a time for celebration with hellebores, snowdrops, and witch hazels (*Hamamelis*) delivering sparkling highlights on cold days. The choices increase as spring and summer arrive, while shade-loving trees and shrubs that produce berries will brighten up gloomy areas through the fall.

Combine hellebores and snowdrops beneath deciduous trees to color up your yard in late winter.

Tender begonias, coleus, and ginger lilies, plus hardy Japanese anemones, add a tropical note in summer.

CREATE A TROPICAL PARADISE

Tender plants, including begonias, coleus (*Solenostemon*), and ginger lilies (*Hedychium*) can transform a gloomy yard into a tropical paradise during the summer months. Supplement them with leafy houseplants such as the umbrella tree (*Schefflera*), jade plant (*Crassula ovata*), and aspidistras that will enjoy the humidity outside in summer and help create a jungle ambience. Keep all these plants in pots with drainage holes in the base, which will make them easier to move back inside when temperatures drop in the fall.

JUST ADD WATER

A still pool will help reflect light into a shady space, as well as doubling the impact of the marginal and bog plants around the edges. Make a small pond in part shade, a few yards away from the canopies of large deciduous trees; high volumes of fall leaves can pollute the water when they drop in and start to decompose. Good choices of flowering and foliage plants for the damp soil next to a pond include candelabra primulas, ferns, hostas, and rodgersias.

The jewel colors of candelabra primulas, hostas, and ferns are reflected in this tiny woodland pond.

ASSESSING YOUR SHADY YARD

Before embarking on a new design or introducing planting into your landscaping, plot the areas where the sun filters through during the day and those that receive no natural light. Testing your soil will also pay dividends; the type you have will determine which plants will thrive in it. These simple checks will help you locate the most suitable positions for seating areas, storage, and water features, too. Hard landscaping choices are also important in shady spaces, where damp, porous surfaces can lead to moss and algae growth, making them slippery and potentially dangerous.

MAPPING LIGHT AND SHADE

Few yards experience uniform levels of light falling on them throughout the day, and areas of sun and shade also change with the seasons, so it's worth mapping out the brightest and darkest spaces at different times of the day and throughout the year.

This will pay dividends when designing seating and dining areas and choosing appropriate plants (see pp.26–27). No special equipment is needed—just a compass or mobile phone will enable you to create a plan of the light levels in your yard.

Use a compass or your phone to discover which direction your yard faces.

THE RIGHT DIRECTION

The direction your yard faces, known as its aspect, will largely determine the amount of sunlight it receives each day. For example, a south-facing yard in the northern hemisphere will generally receive bright sunlight for most of the day during the summer months, while a north-facing plot will be mainly in shade. East- and west-facing yards will receive direct sun in the mornings and evenings respectively. However, remember that there may be other features affecting light levels and casting shade over your plot, so take these into account, too (see pp.10–11).

To discover your yard's aspect, simply stand with your back to the house and use a compass.

USE YOUR EYES

The simplest way to locate areas of sun and shade is just to note where the sun strikes your yard in the morning, at midday, in the afternoon, and again in the evening. Taking photos will help you remember the exact spots that are sunny or shady at different times, allowing you to match them with suitable plants and perhaps design a space for morning coffee and another for evening drinks. You may find that a seemingly shady yard has areas where the sun shines for as much as six hours per day, which could broaden your plant choices for those spots (see pp.12–13).

Also assess the light levels at different times of the year, since they will vary quite considerably, with shade often increasing in winter when the sun is low in the sky. This may not be a problem for perennial plants that die down in the fall, but it could affect evergreens that need light throughout the year. However, areas beneath deciduous trees that lose their leaves in the fall may be brighter in winter, allowing you to include some cold-season flowering plants to decorate those spaces.

Pinpoint areas that receive a few hours of sun for a raised bed, where you can grow a few leafy crops such as lettuces.

INCREASING THE LIGHT

In dark spaces beneath evergreen shrubs or trees with dense canopies, you can increase the light by removing some of the lower branches. Known as "lifting the canopy," this can allow more sun to flood the yard (see pp.28–29).

Removing the lower branches of a tree or large shrub allows more light to penetrate to the planting below.

Photograph your yard at different times of the day to map out areas of light and shade.

ASSESSING YOUR
YARD CONDITIONS

To create a beautifully planted shady yard with sheltered seating and dining areas, it is important to carry out a few checks before you begin. Having assessed the light and shade (*see pp.22–23*), now take a closer look at your soil, which will determine your planting options. The climate, average rainfall, wind direction, and your specific conditions (microclimate) will also influence your designs.

Frost travels downhill and causes most damage to plants growing at the bottom of a slope.

TESTING YOUR SOIL

There are various different soil types, and the conditions each creates affect plant growth. Most soils have a high percentage of either sand or clay particles, or yours may be a loam that contains optimum levels of both sand and clay that many plants enjoy.

Sandy soils consist of relatively large particles, rather like the grains on a beach. Water drains quickly through the spaces between the particles, which makes these soils quite dry. They are also relatively infertile because plant nutrients, which are held in a solution of water, wash away when it rains. Sandy soils are known as "light" because they are easy to dig.

Clay soils comprise minute particles that trap moisture and plant nutrients in the tiny spaces between them. These dense soils are prone to waterlogging in winter and the surfaces can become hard and cracked during prolonged dry spells. They are known as "heavy" because they are difficult to dig, but clays are fertile and many plants thrive when grown in them.

The balance of sand, clay, and silt in loams facilitates enough water retention for plants' roots to soak it up, while allowing any excess to drain away, and

Spreading a layer of homemade compost will improve a soil's structure while suppressing weed growth and preventing erosion.

they are often referred to as moist but well-drained soils. While loams generally support the widest range of plants, a vast number are adapted to other types, so it's simply a case of matching your soil

with plants that like it. To check your soil type, remove a small sample from just below the surface. Leave it to dry off until just damp, and then rub it between your fingers to feel its texture.

TYPES OF SOIL

SANDY SOIL feels gritty when rubbed between the fingers. If you try to mold a damp sample of sandy soil into a ball or sausage shape, it will fall apart.

CLAY SOIL feels smooth, dense, and sticky to the touch. It will retain its shape when molded into a sausage shape or ball, and if it has a very high clay content, it will not break apart even when bent into a horseshoe shape.

LOAMS include a variety of soils, some with higher proportions of sand, which feel a little gritty, others with more clay that are smoother. Both may form a ball when rolled but they won't feel sticky nor have such a defined shape as clay.

PROTECTION FROM THE ELEMENTS

If you have been living in your region for a while, you will probably already know something about the local climate, be that a frost-free but windy coastal area, a cold inland region prone to snow, or a place where little rain falls in summer. When choosing plants, first check that they can tolerate these local conditions, and then take a closer look at your own specific plot. Shade will inevitably reduce the temperatures in summer, but if the trees and shrubs causing it also protect your yard from cold winds, it may feel warmer than more exposed sites at other times of the year. The topography will also affect temperatures—hilltops tend to be cold and windy, while frost travels downhill and collects in low-lying areas known as "frost pockets," which can be even colder.

Cold air can also become trapped behind solid barriers such as walls, fences, and dense evergreen hedging, which may also increase wind turbulence. To create a sheltered area, erect a semipermeable screen, which will slow down the wind speed and protect the area behind and in front of it. A barrier that allows about 50 percent of the air to pass through, such as a deciduous hedge, woven hurdle, or trellis is best.

> **TOP TIP** TO IDENTIFY THE FROST POCKETS IN YOUR YARD, AFTER A COLD NIGHT, NOTE THE AREAS WHERE PLANTS ARE COVERED IN A HEAVY LAYER OF FROST AND THOSE THAT HAVE ESCAPED IT.

A woven willow fence protects planting from strong wind and may also allow some light through.

MEASURING SOIL ACIDITY

The measure of a soil's acidity or alkalinity is known as its pH value. Most plants enjoy neutral to slightly acid conditions but some, including rhododendrons, camellias, and pieris, grow well only in acid soils, while lavender, clematis and rock roses prefer alkaline conditions. You may find acid-loving plants listed as lime-hating or lime-intolerant. Kits for testing soil pH are inexpensive to buy at a garden center—very easy to use, they will quickly identify your soil type.

Camellias prefer acid soil and their leaves will turn yellow when they are grown in ground that is alkaline.

CREATING A LANDSCAPE PLAN

Itemizing features in your yard such as sheds, patios, and flowerbeds and noting their locations will help you identify those that may need removing or replacing to allow in more light where needed. Your **inventory can then be added to a simple landscape plan that will help you redesign the whole yard or parts of it, maximizing its potential. To create a plan, plot the length, width, and diagonal lengths of your space.**

An online landscape design program provides a simple way to make a scale plan of your yard.

FIRST THINGS FIRST

Making a plan that includes the existing features in your yard will provide you with a visual map of what you have to work with. This can be a pencil sketch of your plot, roughly to scale, on graph paper, or you can generate a plan by putting the yard's dimensions and the size and location of the features into an online landscape design program. Then make copies on which to show the areas of light and shade throughout the year.

Next, think about what you need in the space. Writing a list of your requirements will help you decide what to keep, relocate, or remove to maximize light levels and make best use of your outdoor space.

Your wish list may include spaces for seating and dining; shady play areas for children; increased privacy; storage space for bikes, tools, and furniture; beds to grow crops; and a small pond for wildlife.

MAKE A NEW PLAN

Checking off points on your wish list that marry up with features you already have in the yard allows you to see clearly what's missing. Also list anything that is currently not in the best position (see also pp.10–11). Then make a new plan with your ideal layout for the space where, for example, seating is in shade at midday in summer, storage sheds are not throwing the yard into deep shade, and boundaries are providing privacy without blocking all the light.

While some fruits and vegetables can cope with part shade, few will tolerate dark areas, so choose the brightest patch for an edible plot (see pp.122–123). A pond is best installed in part shade (see pp.46–47), while planting beds can be included wherever you need an injection of foliage and flower color. With such a wide range of beautiful planting options, a bed in shade won't be a problem, but remember that choices will be more limited in areas of deep shade, especially if the soil is also dry.

Established trees are best left in situ wherever possible (see pp.10–11), and consider the location of new ones carefully—ensure they will provide shade where it's needed and won't undermine the foundations of your home (see pp.80–81).

Photographing the space from an upstairs window can help you assess areas that need redesigning.

A bench in a partly shaded area surrounded by plants that like low light will offer a relaxing place to sit on a hot summer's day.

RAISING THE ROOF

An easy way to increase planting or seating spaces in a shady yard is to raise the canopy of a tree or shrub. This simply entails removing some of the low-growing stems to create an area beneath that is exposed to more light. Before pruning, check online or with staff at a tree nursery for the best months to cut your plant, since some bleed sap or are more prone to disease if trimmed at the wrong time of year. Also ensure your tools are clean and sharp and wear sturdy gloves to prevent injuries.

HOW TO RAISE A CANOPY

YOU WILL NEED Sturdy gardening gloves
• Sharp pruners • Pruning saw

1 Select a tree or shrub that is casting
shade over the yard, with branches
formed all along the trunk or main
stem. This evergreen bay tree is a
good example. It has grown above the
height of the boundary fence and
the lower stems are now blocking the
sun from reaching the soil below it.

2 Pull back the foliage to expose the
main trunk or stems so you can
assess what will need to be removed.
You are aiming to produce a plant
with a clear lower stem and leafy
canopy above.

3 Wear gloves and use a sharp pruning
saw to remove the lower branches,
starting at the bottom of the plant.
Remove heavy stems in stages to
avoid them snapping or tearing and
take care not to cut too close to the
main trunk, which may expose the
plant to disease (*see pp.134–135*).

4 Continue to remove branches until
you have a clear stem or trunk,
with space beneath the canopy for
a planting bed or a seat. In this
east-facing yard, the area will
receive light for a few hours in the
morning in the summer when the
sun is at a low angle.

> **TOP TIP** KEEP AN EYE OUT FOR NEW
> SHOOTS THAT MAY SPROUT FROM THE
> LOWER TRUNK OR STEMS OF A PRUNED
> TREE OR SHRUB AND RUB THEM OFF
> WITH YOUR FINGERS AS SOON AS YOU
> SEE THEM.

The lower stems of this Tibetan
cherry (*opposite*) were removed in
summer to allow more light onto
the beds below.

MAKE A LOLLIPOP

In a more open area, you could take
this technique further and shape the
canopy as well to create a lollipop-
headed tree, where light will filter
in all around it to the planting below.
Just remember that to maintain this
elegant shape, the tree will require
annual clipping in early summer
and you may need to call in a tree
surgeon or arborist to do the work if
it grows too tall for you to reach the
top without balancing on a ladder.

Bay trees are shade-tolerant and
relatively easy to trim into a beautiful
round-headed topiary feature.

DESIGNING A SHADY SPACE

Taking time to plan your shady landscaping carefully will help you design the perfect outdoor space for your needs. Identify the best places for seating and planting and think about how you can make the most of each area by adding focal points to catch the eye and furniture that is both beautiful and practical. Reassessing your boundaries might also allow more light into the yard without compromising privacy, and making a feature of the dark, sunless areas will bring even the gloomiest spots to life.

PLANNING BEDS AND BORDERS

After making a design plan of your yard (*see pp.26–27*) and pinpointing the best areas for planting, you now have to decide on the size and shape of your beds and borders. To achieve a show of flowers and foliage all year round, you will need space for a selection of different types of plants, while making sure that the conditions in the yard meet their needs. To create a beautiful display, simply follow these tips.

Make borders as large as possible and fill with layers of planting that perform at different times of the year.

BIG IS BEST

While it may be tempting in a small space to create skinny beds that hug the boundaries, they will provide space for only a few plants, which could leave gaps or bare stems when they have finished flowering or lost their leaves in winter. In a shady yard, this problem may be exacerbated as the whole border could be plunged into shadow from late fall to early spring if it is next to a

wall or fence, even if it receives some sunlight for the rest of the year. The soil next to a boundary can also be in a rain shadow, resulting in dry shade—the most challenging of all planting conditions.

The answer to these problems is to be brave and mark out borders that are at least 3 ft (1 m) in depth. This will allow you to fit in layers of evergreen and deciduous plants, such as trees, shrubs, and perennial flowers that perform at

different times and collectively produce a continuous show (*see p.51*). This design solution will make the yard look bigger, too—masking the boundaries with leaves and flowers fools the eye into thinking the space is larger than its actual dimensions. Also consider bringing some of the planting into the center of your space, where there may be more light.

Creating beds in the center of a small space can help to make it look bigger.

BOLD SHAPES

The shape of a border can also enhance the design effect. Try squares; rectangles; ovals; circles; or broad, sweeping curves, rather than amorphous shapes or beds with wiggly or zigzagged lines, which often just look messy after the plants start to creep over the edges.

Design the shape of a lawn in relation to your beds. Bold geometric shapes also look best for areas of turf, with the borders fitting around them to create a neat pattern. Either draw out the shapes on your plan or take a photo from an upstairs window, print it out and sketch in your proposed beds, borders, and lawns (see also pp.38–39).

Installing raised beds in a gloomy area will lift up the plants, offering them a little more light.

RAISING LEVELS

Where the soil at ground level is in deep shade, consider installing raised beds if they will allow more light to reach your plants and thereby widen your choices. Simple wooden beds are relatively cheap but some last only a few years, so you may wish to opt for more expensive hardwood features made from oak or another durable material; if possible, select large beds, which may need watering less frequently than smaller types. Remember to factor in the cost of filling them with topsoil or potting mix, too.

Set your raised beds directly on the soil or, if installing one on a patio, remove a few pavers under it to allow moisture to drain freely into the ground. A bed installed on a solid surface will leak muddy water from the base or could become waterlogged.

Carve out beds with sweeping curved edges to create drama in a small space.

TOP TIP YOU CAN EASILY EXTEND THE SIZE OR CHANGE THE SHAPE OF EXISTING BEDS, BUT REMEMBER THAT TREES AND LARGE SHRUBS WHICH WERE PLANTED MORE THAN FIVE YEARS EARLIER MAY NOT SURVIVE TRANSPLANTING SO TRY TO WORK AROUND THEM IF YOU CAN.

MAKING SPACES FOR SEATING AND DINING

The location of patios, terraces, and other seating areas to create relaxing, comfortable spaces requires careful planning. The ideal area for sitting or dining may not be close to the house, especially if it is in deep shade or exposed to wind, while a spot farther away may offer more light and shelter. You can also augment seating areas with plants and design features to enhance your enjoyment.

Plan seating areas that offer a good view while you enjoy cool shade at midday in summer.

LOCATE THE SWEET SPOTS

In design terms, a sweet spot for sitting or dining is where optimal light and shelter provide cool shade during the heat of the day in summer, while capturing some of the weaker sun rays in the morning or evening and during cooler seasons. Having assessed your conditions, you now know where the areas of sun and shade are, and if you have a frost pocket or windy site (*see pp.22–27*), which will help you to pinpoint the ideal places for seating. If the yard is large enough, consider more than one seating area to make the most of the sun and to view your design from different angles.

As with beds and borders, size is important when planning a seating or dining area. For areas that need to accommodate a family and a few friends or offer space to stretch out on a sunbed, first measure the size of the furniture you are planning to include and then calculate the size of the area required. It must be large enough for the table and for you to push back a chair to get up without it tipping into a flowerbed or scraping the surface off the lawn. Then add about 18 in (45 cm) to this measurement to allow space to walk around the furniture.

Look for areas with morning or late afternoon sun for casual seating such as a bench or bistro set.

If you are including a few other smaller seating areas, consider a patio set within a bed or border that is shaded for most of the day but traps the morning or evening sun. Make the area just big enough for two chairs and a coffee or bistro table where you can unwind in cool shade at midday and enjoy breakfast or evening drinks surrounded by flowers and foliage, with just enough sun to warm you.

MAKING ADJUSTMENTS

Not all yards offer the perfect spots for relaxing, and an existing patio may be too expensive to move. In this case, you may be able to remove features such as sheds or cut back plants to improve the conditions. For example, where a tree is casting deep shade, try taking off some of the lower branches to allow more light through (see pp.28–29). If the tree is in a neighboring yard you could discuss with the owner if this would be possible and offer to pay for the work.

It may also be possible to prune back other plants or remove them to allow light onto a patio. Take your time when pruning, since a plant may take a long time to regrow if you remove too much.

Wind turbulence often occurs behind solid walls and fences, so replacing these with more open structures that allow air to pass through (see p.25) may alleviate the problem. In an open, windy site, try planting a deciduous hedge or tall perennial plants and grasses that will reduce the wind speed and make the area more comfortable, without casting too much shade.

Removing a few plants that are blocking the sun could create beautiful dappled sunlight on a seating area.

A log pile in a quiet, shady corner will attract a host of wildlife such as beetles and chipmunks.

DEALING WITH DARK CORNERS

Areas of deep shade where it is too cool to sit can be used for storage to house seat cushions or gardening tools, or for a statue or ornament that will sing out from the darkness. Alternatively, use it for a pile of logs, which will invite beetles and hibernating animals to set up home there. Moss may grow in these corners, covering the ground with a spongy bright green carpet in cool, damp spots—look up Japanese stroll gardens for ideas on how to use mossy surfaces to create a beautiful design effect.

CHOOSING MATERIALS

When you are choosing landscaping materials and furniture for a shady yard, pale colors will help reflect light into the gloom—but remember that these may also show the dirt more easily, so check how easy they are to clean. Safety is another priority for areas of high foot traffic, so look for materials that will not be slippery when wet. Cost may also be a factor. There is a wide range of paving and furniture to suit most pockets and you could minimize the expense and lower your carbon footprint, too, by using recycled paving and secondhand furniture from local freecycle websites.

Angular gravel in mixed colors creates a decorative nonslip informal path for a shady space.

STEP ON IT

The choice of hard landscaping materials for patios, terraces, and paths is vast, but before buying there are a few factors to consider for areas in shade. The first is safety. Shady spots are often wet and slippery for long periods after rain, which also creates the perfect conditions for moss and algae growth. Traditional stone and concrete paving stones are prone to mossy growth and will need to be cleaned with a power washer in spring and again on a regular basis when in use to make them safe to walk on. However, some natural hard stone paving and porcelain tiles are less porous and generally safer, since this also makes them more resistant to moss and algae growth. Alternatively, you could use reclaimed stones to create crazy paving and make a feature of moss growing in the cracks—the small, irregular stones will make the surface less slippery underfoot than a smoother finish, but you may still need to remove some moss from time to time.

Natural timber decking can also be quite hazardous when wet, so if this is the look you want to create, consider nonslip composite decking to make the surface safer. Some decking products contain plastic—look for those that use only natural or recycled materials if you want to minimize the polluting effects on the environment.

Gravel offers an easy-care option for paths or informal seating areas. Moss and algae do not grow as easily on the small stones, while 0.4 or 0.6 in (10 or 14 mm) angular gravel is the most comfortable to walk on. Pale shades reflect light back into the space, but avoid white gravel for patios and paths because it gets dirty easily and may look too stark. Add edging to keep gravel in place and a few pavers under furniture legs.

Recycled cobbles and pavers create a textured patio where moss can be left to grow between the cracks.

Outdoor sofa cushions may be weather-resistant but they will still need to be stored indoors in winter.

SELECTING FURNITURE FOR SHADE

If left outside in a shady spot all year, some wooden furniture may develop moss or algae and will need to be cleaned before use, although hard wood is generally unaffected. Alternatively, choose items with stainless steel, powder-coated aluminum, or faux rattan (plastic) frames, which are resistant to algal growth and will withstand most weather conditions unharmed.

The good news about shade is that accompanying cushions for sofas and chairs will retain their original fabric colors for longer in areas of low light. However, most are best stored indoors during the winter, even if the manufacturer claims that the fabric is weatherproof, so make sure that you have adequate storage space before buying. Pale colors will reflect more light, but dark colors are less likely to show stains and you can add a few vibrant throw cushions and blankets to brighten them up.

In areas of deep shade, you may wish to consider foldable chairs or a small bistro set that will allow you to take refuge from strong sun during a hot summer but can then be moved to a brighter, warmer spot at other times.

TOP TIP SEATING UNDER A TREE WILL KEEP YOU COOL ON A HOT SUMMER'S DAY, BUT IF BIRDS PERCH ON THE BRANCHES, BUY A LARGE PARASOL OR USE A SAIL TO PROTECT YOU AND YOUR FURNITURE FROM THE INEVITABLE DROPPINGS.

LAWNS FOR SHADY SPACES

Most lawn grasses need four to six hours of direct sunlight each day to thrive, so if you want to sod a shady yard you need to use a type designed for low-light areas or opt for a carpet of suitable ground cover plants instead. The latter is the best solution for areas under trees with dense canopies that cast deep shade during the summer—their roots may also out-compete grasses for water and essential nutrients.

Choose a shade-tolerant grass mix for areas under trees and mow less frequently than you would a lawn in sun.

Use a bark chip mulch around a tree with a dense canopy where turf would fail to grow.

CHOOSING GRASS FOR SHADE

When sodding or seeding a lawn in a shady space, select a mix that is designed specifically for low-light conditions. In dry areas beneath trees or in yards that have free-draining soils, choose one that has a high proportion of fescue grasses; if you are planning a lawn in damp shade, opt for a mix that contains bent grasses (*Agrostis*).

To ensure lawn seed germinates under a deciduous tree, sow in late fall after the leaves have dropped or in early spring before the canopy unfurls. The extra light at these times will encourage germination and more vigorous plant growth, as long as temperatures remain above 41°F (5°C).

Do not lay sod or sow seed too close to trees, since the additional competition for water and nutrients will compromise the health of the tree, as well as limiting the grass growth. Leave a circle of 3 ft (1 m) in diameter around trees, particularly if they are young or newly planted, and cover the ground with bark chips to suppress weed growth, leaving a small gap so they do not touch the trunks.

CARING FOR A SHADED LAWN

Grass grows more slowly in shade, so mow your lawn less frequently and raise the cutting height to 2½–3½ in (6–9 cm), which will help it cope better during periods of drought. Don't worry if the lawn turns brown in hot, dry weather as it will soon recover when rain returns.

In areas under trees with dense canopies, where the soil remains dry through the summer, even after rain, consider using drought-tolerant ground cover instead of grass. Good choices include the barren strawberry (*Waldsteinia ternata*), which has pretty yellow flowers and decorative strawberry-like leaves, snowy wood rush (*Luzula nivea*), and woodruff (*Galium odoratum*) (see pp.40–41).

Use a fall lawn food that's rich in potassium (K) each year, applying it just before the trees lose their leaves. Feed again in spring, using a fertilizer designed for this time of year, and apply half the recommended dose.

Raising the cutting height when mowing lawns in shade will help the grass withstand periods of drought.

Barren strawberry (*Waldsteinia ternata*) is a colorful alternative to grass for areas in dry shade.

LAWN ALTERNATIVES

Ground cover plants adapted to woodland habitats make good lawn substitutes and will spread across the soil in shady areas to produce a decorative carpet of leaves and flowers. Most are not suitable to be walked on regularly but, like a lawn, evergreen plants create a lush green effect throughout the year. Most need no mowing and little or no additional fertilizer once established, taking the pressure off you to maintain them, while also causing less damage to the environment (see pp.40–41).

You may be tempted to lay artificial grass in areas of shade, but remember that it will contribute to plastic pollution and provides no benefits for pollinators or other garden wildlife.

GROUND COVER FOR SHADE

If you're looking for a lawn alternative to decorate areas close to trees and shrubs or other shady spots, these low-growing plants will produce a textured carpet of foliage, flowers, and, in some cases, colorful berries. Unlike grass, which needs regular mowing, they require very little maintenance once established and are an excellent choice for those with little time on their hands. While they won't tolerate high foot traffic, many support pollinators and wildlife as well as, or better than, grass. Just check that your soil matches their requirements before buying.

GRAY SEDGE *CAREX DIVULSA*

HEIGHT AND SPREAD 16 × 16 in (40 × 40 cm)
SOIL Well-drained; moist but well-drained
HARDINESS Fully hardy
SUN ☀ ☀

This evergreen offers a beautiful substitute for lawn turf, its fountains of dark green or grayish-green leaves creating a colorful carpet when planted en masse. Small, pale yellow flowers appear in spring. Tolerant of part shade and well-drained soils, it will grow well at the edges of a tree canopy or in a more open site. Rake out dead leaves and flowers in spring and trim plants back after flowering to encourage fresh growth. This sedge may turn brown in harsh winters but will recover in spring.

The gray sedge's evergreen grasslike foliage makes a good substitute for a regular lawn.

BEARBERRY *ARCTOSTAPHYLOS UVA-URSI*

HEIGHT AND SPREAD 4 × 20 in (10 × 50 cm)
SOIL Moist but well-drained; acid
HARDINESS Fully hardy
SUN ☀ ☀

The leathery evergreen foliage of this diminutive, spreading shrub delivers year-round interest, carpeting the ground with small, dark green leaves. In spring, the new shoots are flushed with red, while small, pink, urn-shaped flowers add dots of color when they appear in summer. The blooms are followed by red berries in the fall. If you have the acid soil this shrub demands (see p.25), it is easy to grow and maintain—simply apply a mulch of well-rotted leaf mold around the plants in the fall or spring.

Bright red berries appear in the fall over dark green leaves and persist into the winter.

CREEPING DOGWOOD *CORNUS CANADENSIS*

HEIGHT AND SPREAD 4 × 36 in (10 × 90 cm)
SOIL Well-drained; moist but well-drained; neutral to acid
HARDINESS Fully hardy
SUN ☀ ☀

The dainty white flowers of the spreading dogwood create an eye-catching feature when they push up between the leaf rosettes in late spring and early summer. Made up of petal-like bracts with small greenish-yellow flowers in the center, they precede the red berries that appear in late summer. The green foliage also turns wine-red in the fall. This deciduous perennial will cover the ground in lightly shaded areas, but check first that you have the neutral to acid soil it needs.

Small white flowers create a dotted pattern in late spring when they emerge from the center of the leaf rosettes.

WOODRUFF *GALIUM ODORATUM*

HEIGHT AND SPREAD 6 × 18 in (15 × 45 cm)
SOIL Well-drained; moist but well-drained
HARDINESS Fully hardy
SUN ☀

The divided leaves of this perennial look like little stars when they unfurl in spring, and quickly cover the ground beneath trees and shrubs. They release a light scent when crushed but do not tolerate heavy foot traffic. In late spring, tiny white flowers cover the leaves like a dusting of snow. The dried foliage can be used in teas and jellies, while the edible blooms make decorative garnishes. Requiring almost no maintenance, woodruff spreads via runners and can be kept in check by digging out unwanted growth.

Woodruff's divided leaves appear in spring, just before the tiny flowers open.

SNOWY WOOD RUSH *LUZULA NIVEA*

HEIGHT AND SPREAD 24 × 18 in (60 × 45 cm)
SOIL Well-drained; moist but well-drained
HARDINESS Hardy to 5°F (−15°C)
SUN ☀ ☀

The slim evergreen leaves of the snowy wood rush look like meadow grass and will create a similar effect, even in areas of deep shade. In midsummer, wiry stems of small white fluffy flowers that resemble snowballs appear between the leaves. Plant it en masse to cover swathes of bare soil beneath trees and shrubs, where it will also help suppress weed growth, and deadhead the blooms as soon as they start to fade if you want to prevent it from self-seeding elsewhere.

Named after its fluffy white flowers, the snowy wood rush tolerates all levels of shade.

BLACK LILYTURF *OPHIOPOGON PLANISCAPUS* 'NIGRESCENS'

HEIGHT AND SPREAD 8 × 12 in (20 × 30 cm)
SOIL Moist but well-drained
HARDINESS Fully hardy
SUN ☀ ☀

Ideal for a contemporary garden, the shiny, dark purple to black, bladelike leaves of lilyturf will create graphic effect when used as ground cover. In summer, spikes of small, bell-shaped, pale mauve flowers appear between the leaves, followed in the fall by black berries that endure into winter. This elegant plant will spread slowly to form a leafy mat and needs very little attention once established, apart from adding a mulch of leaf mold in spring to help maintain the moisture in the soil.

Lilyturf's shiny black leaves and mauve flowers create a striking lawn substitute.

JAPANESE SPURGE *PACHYSANDRA TERMINALIS*

HEIGHT AND SPREAD 10 × 36 in (25 × 90 cm)
SOIL Moist but well-drained
HARDINESS Hardy to 5°F (−15°C)
SUN ☀ ☀

The toothed leaves of this creeping evergreen perennial soon spread to form a dense weed-suppressing carpet, while short spikes of small white flowers provide additional interest when they appear in early summer. Alternatively, you can choose the cultivar 'Variegata' to brighten gloomy areas with its sparkling pale gold-edged foliage. Perfect for covering the soil under deciduous trees and shrubs where few other plants will thrive, this easygoing plant requires little aftercare once established.

Low rosettes of tooth-edged green leaves knit together to create an intricately textured carpet.

CREATING BOUNDARIES

Structures and plants that mark the boundaries of a space can enhance its beauty with their colors and textures. While most screens create some shade, you can allow more light in by using airy planting or see-through structures such as a trellis. Consider minimizing the height of boundaries where privacy is not needed, and use durable materials in deep, damp shade where structures may be more vulnerable to rotting.

Leaving small gaps between fencing posts creates a shelter belt and allows slices of light to penetrate into the space.

FENCES AND WALLS

Shade cast by boundary fencing and walls can be a blessing or a curse, depending on where it falls and how much of the space it affects. You can let in more light by using open-weave slatted fencing or trellis to mark your boundary where privacy is not an issue. These will also allow more air to filter through, which helps create a shelter belt by reducing wind turbulence behind them. Greater airflow means they tend to dry out relatively quickly after rain, too, making some types more durable than solid softwood fences.

Old brick and stone walls can develop beautiful patinas in shady spaces, where mosses and ferns take hold in cracks in the pointing and lichens develop on the surfaces. Just check periodically that the pointing has not been undermined and that your wall is structurally sound.

Painted fencing and trellis help to lighten this space dominated by a large, imposing building at the back.

Colorful hardy fuchsias make beautiful deciduous hedging plants for a sheltered, shady space.

HEDGES AND PLANTS

If you are considering a hedge to define a shady boundary, make sure that the plants you choose will tolerate low-light conditions. Good choices for evergreens include yew (*Taxus baccata*), Lawson's cypress (*Chamaecyparis lawsoniana*), holly (*Ilex*), spotted laurel (*Aucuba*), and Portugal laurel (*Prunus lusitanica*). Alternatively, opt for a deciduous hedge, which will allow more light into the space in winter. Hawthorn (*Crataegus monogyna*), fuchsia (*Fuchsia magellanica*), guelder rose (*Viburnum opulus*), hornbeam (*Carpinus betulus*), and beech (*Fagus*) are suitable options for shady sites—the latter two retain all or some of their crisp, golden fall foliage throughout winter.

In areas where privacy is not needed, consider a boundary line made up of low-growing shrubs and perennials (see pp.58–73) that will inject color and interest throughout the year.

OPTIMUM HEIGHTS FOR BOUNDARIES

The maximum legal height for a boundary wall or fence will vary depending on where you live. You may prefer a lower solid structure with a trellis panel on top to allow in more light while still offering privacy. The height for boundaries that face a road is likely to be around 3 ft (1 m), but a lower structure may be enough to deter pedestrians from entering while allowing you to choose from a greater range of plants. Including a variety of trees, shrubs, and flowering plants in a front yard not only boosts biodiversity but can also prevent localized flooding, so it is a good idea to green up this valuable space, however small it is.

Woven hazel hurdles create a low, see-through screen that allows some light to filter through to the plants.

INTRODUCING WATER

Reflecting sparkles of light into areas of shade, a pond or water feature will brighten up a space and also bring a host of additional benefits. Aquatic and bog plants provide color and texture, boosting biodiversity, and amphibians such as frogs and toads will quickly find an expanse of open water to breed. Ponds and pools also draw in birds, small mammals, and insects to drink and bathe, while fountains and bubbling water features introduce a tranquil soundscape.

A pond reflects light into a shady space and also animates it with the birds and wildlife that the water attracts.

Moving water creates a tranquil atmosphere, the soothing sounds inducing relaxation.

CHOOSING A FEATURE

From reflective ponds and barrel pools to plug-in-and-play fountains and bubbling features for patios and balconies, there are water features for every yard size and budget. The smaller self-contained units that simply plug into an outdoor electricity supply can be installed in areas of quite deep shade, since the moving water helps prevent algae growth, although they will still need to be cleaned from time to time. Other fountain features that comprise a few elements, such as a pump and decorative unit that sits on top of a reservoir, are also suitable for shady spaces and relatively easy to install. Alternatively, you could opt for a rill. These long, shallow channels can be used to divide different areas of the yard, and they also include a pump to keep the water moving, which helps prevent algae from growing.

CREATING A POND

A pond containing plants will need sufficient light to sustain pond and bog species, few of which tolerate full shade. Install a pond where part of the surface is in sun and part in shade, which will help moderate fluctuations in the water temperature and subsequent weed and algae growth, while providing ideal conditions for a wide range of plants. Also site it away from deciduous trees that would deposit large numbers of leaves in the water in the fall; they would pollute it when they decompose.

Look online for tutorials on how to install a pond or barrel pool, and plan the size and shape of your feature carefully. To encourage wildlife, make a shallow slope along one side to allow birds and other creatures to access the water. If you are making a feature in a barrel or large container that isn't sunk into the ground, add a plank of wood or pots around it to allow them to get in and out.

Create sloping sides to the pond to allow birds to drink and bathe at a depth that suits them.

Even small ponds will attract wildlife, but aim for a depth of 12–24 in (24–60 cm) and create shelves around the edge to accommodate plants that prefer just their toes in the water and others that like their roots submerged. You can also make a bog garden by lining a hole in the ground with a waterproof liner and making a few holes in it for drainage. Backfill with the excavated soil and, once planted, add a thick mulch over the surface to trap moisture in the ground.

PLANTING A POND

The best wildlife-friendly ponds include a diverse range of plants, from marginals such as marsh marigold (*Caltha palustris*), water forget-me-not (*Myosotis scorpioides*), and arum lilies (*Zantedeschia*) that live in the shallow water around the edges, to aquatics such as hornwort (*Ceratophyllum demersum*) and spatterdock (*Nuphar lutea*), the roots and leaves of which grow below the surface. Not all will thrive in shade, so use those on pp.46–47 or check labels to ensure they will be happy in your pond. Plant them in pond baskets or bags in aquatic potting mix—regular mix is too rich in nutrients and will promote algae and weed growth.

Plant aquatics in pond bags or baskets filled with aquatic potting mix and topped with pebbles or gravel.

A nontoxic black dye has been added to the water of this modern feature to keep it clear of weeds.

CLEAR VIEW

Plants absorb many of the nutrients that pond weeds need to thrive, so packing your pond with a good range of marginals and noninvasive deep-water aquatics will help keep the water clear. Duckweed and some algae may still develop, so fish them out with a net now and again, and leave the debris on the sides of the pond for a day or two to allow any pond creatures you have removed some time to return to the water.

In reflective bowls or tanks, you could try adding black dye formulated for water features to keep them clear. This blocks out the sunlight needed by weeds to photosynthesize and grow. It is harmless to wildlife and to plants with leaves and flowers that grow above the surface.

POND PLANTS FOR SHADE

The choice of water-loving plants that tolerate shade is not huge, but there are a few stalwarts guaranteed to brighten up your pond. Some favorites such as Japanese water irises (*Iris laevigata*) will bloom in light shade, despite labels often suggesting otherwise, but water lilies and pickerel weed (*Pontederia*) demand more sun and will stubbornly refuse to bloom if their needs are not met. The plants listed here, together with the royal fern *Osmunda regalis* (see *p.115*), represent some of the best options for ponds in part shade.

MARSH MARIGOLD *CALTHA PALUSTRIS*

HEIGHT AND SPREAD 16 × 18 in (40 × 45 cm)
SOIL Moist
HARDINESS Hardy to 5°F (−15°C)
SUN ☼ ☼

The large buttercup-shaped yellow flowers of this plant open in spring when few other marginals are performing, creating a sparkling display over the dark green, kidney-shaped leaves. Grow it at the edges of a pond or in a bog garden close to the water to enjoy the bright flowers reflected in the surface. If the leaves fall over into the water after the plant has bloomed, cut them back to keep it tidy and promote new growth. This plant is not invasive and is ideal for small ponds and shallow streamside settings.

Golden flowers cover the marsh marigold in spring, creating colorful reflections in the water.

MEADOWSWEET *FILIPENDULA* SPECIES

HEIGHT AND SPREAD Up to 5 × 3 ft (1.5 × 1 m)
SOIL Moist
HARDINESS Fully hardy
SUN ☼ ☼

Cultivated species of *Filipendula* enjoy the damp soil conditions in a bog garden, where they will produce sprays of tiny pink or creamy-white flowers over a long period in summer. The architectural, deeply lobed foliage offers added interest before the blooms appear. Choose from *F. ulmaria*, which grows to just 30 in (75 cm) in height, or the taller *F. purpurea*, *F. rubra*, and *F. palmata*, which reach 4 ft (1.2 m) or more. Grown close to the water's edge, filipendulas create a beautiful leafy screen and habitat for frogs and toads.

Filipendula palmata produces fluffy pink flower heads over handsome, deeply lobed foliage.

WATER FORGET-ME-NOT *MYOSOTIS SCORPIOIDES*

HEIGHT AND SPREAD 12 × 16 in (30 × 40 cm)
SOIL Moist
HARDINESS Fully hardy
SUN ☼ ☼

Creating a dainty frill in the shallow water around the edge of a pond, this moisture-loving forget-me-not can also be grown in a bog garden, if the soil remains damp all year round. Spreading via creeping rhizomes, it bears a profusion of small green leaves topped in summer with sprays of tiny bright blue flowers with distinctive yellow eyes. Pink and white varieties are also available. Like its land-based cousin, this plant self-seeds readily, but it is easy to keep under control by pulling out any unwanted growth.

Masses of dainty blue flowers adorn the water forget-me-not from early to midsummer.

CANDELABRA PRIMROSE *PRIMULA* SPECIES

HEIGHT AND SPREAD 18 × 12 in (45 × 30 cm)
SOIL Moist
HARDINESS Fully hardy
SUN ☼ ☼

These eye-catching perennials are ideal for a bog garden, producing broad, crinkly-textured, light green leaves before tall stems of small flowers appear in late spring and early summer. They come in shades of pink, purple, orange, yellow, and white and resemble candelabras, appearing in small clusters along the stems. These colorful plants will bloom for many years with little attention if you provide them with the moist soil they need to thrive. Simply cut back spent flower stems to keep them tidy.

In spring, *Primula japonica* and its hybrids form a colorful pond edge, where they thrive in the damp soil.

RODGERSIA *RODGERSIA* SPECIES

HEIGHT AND SPREAD Up to 4 × 5 ft (1.2 × 1.5 m)
SOIL Moist
HARDINESS Fully hardy
SUN ☼ ☼ ☀

This group of shade-loving perennials thrives in the damp soil beside a natural pond or in a bog garden. Grown for their textured divided foliage and conical spikes of small, fluffy, creamy-white or pink flowers, which appear over a long period in summer, these plants are guaranteed to add impact to your yard if you have space to accommodate them. Among the few pondside plants that will tolerate deep shade, they offer a habitat for amphibians, as well as nectar for bees and other pollinators.

Rodgersia aesculifolia sports large, textured leaves and sprays of tiny white summer flowers.

WATER FIGWORT *SCROPHULARIA AURICULATA* 'VARIEGATA'

HEIGHT AND SPREAD 3 × 2 ft (90 × 60 cm)
SOIL Moist
HARDINESS Fully hardy
SUN ☼

This leafy marginal perennial will decorate the water's edge from spring to fall, when its tall, square stems of cream-edged green foliage appear. It also produces small brown flowers that offer little decorative value but are loved by bees. Water figwort makes a good foil for more colorful pond and bog plants, and offers cover for amphibians and other water creatures. It performs reliably each year with little maintenance, but may self-seed a little too enthusiastically if the spent flowers are not removed.

The decorative variegated leaves of this water figwort create a foil for colorful aquatic flowers.

ARUM LILY *ZANTEDESCHIA AETHIOPICA*

HEIGHT AND SPREAD Up to 3 × 2 ft (90 × 60 cm)
SOIL Moist
HARDINESS Hardy to 14°F (−10°C)
SUN ☼ ☼

Prized for its elegant flower heads comprising a white petal-like spathe and spiky yellow spadix, this perennial also produces clumps of sculptural arrow-shaped leaves. Grow it in the shallows at the edges of a pond or in a bog garden where the large blooms will form in succession from spring to summer. This species is the hardiest of the arums; other forms are available in a range of jewel-like shades, but these will need to be lifted and given protection from frost indoors over winter.

Graceful white flower heads appear above this lily's foliage for many weeks in summer.

PLANTING IN A
SHADY YARD

Browsing through this chapter will open your eyes to the vast array of plants that enjoy life in the shade, dispelling any myths about sunless yards offering no flower interest. While it is true that many large, showy blooms enjoy sun, the smaller, more demure woodland flowers have equal charm, and can still pack a punch if you have space to include them in large groups. Also consider foliage plants; their leaves endure longer than flowers and knit together to create a lush, textured carpet.

CHOOSING AND USING SHADE-LOVING PLANTS

Lush foliage and bright flowers can transform a gloomy yard into a space filled with color, texture, and scent. Seasonal plants provide ever-changing drama as the year progresses, while a backbone of trees and shrubs provides permanent structure and interest during the colder months. But before you rush out to the garden center or order online, take time to plan your planting carefully.

Foliage colors and textures deliver a longer season of interest than flowers that come and go.

RIGHT PLANT, RIGHT PLACE

When drawing up a wish list for plants to add to your yard, make sure that their needs are consistent with the conditions in your outside space. Assess the light levels throughout the day (see pp.12–13) and note the local climatic conditions—some parts of your yard may be drier and windier than others. Get to know your soil, too—is it heavy clay, loamy or sandy, or maybe acidic? You can find out by asking local gardeners, or doing a simple soil pH test available from any garden center (see p.25).

Carry out an audit of the existing planting, and make a list of what you would like to save or move. Trees and shrubs may be plunging your space into deep shade, but think carefully before cutting them down. They make a positive contribution to the environment and may be masking eyesores, shielding an ugly view or increasing your privacy, while judicious pruning may be all that's needed to let in more light. Smaller shrubs and flowers can be transplanted, usually in spring or fall, if they are in the wrong place.

Candelabra and purple vial primroses are exacting in their requirements and need moist, acid soil and part shade.

Create layers of planting, with a skirt of perennials and bulbs beneath shrubs such as this Ludlow's tree peony (*Paeonia ludlowii*).

PLANTING IN LAYERS

To create a lush landscape that offers color and texture, try layering your planting. Mature trees and large shrubs form the upper layer and provide height and structure—combine evergreens and deciduous plants that offer seasonal interest. In the spaces below and adjacent to these large plants, use shade-loving perennials (*see pp.66–73*) that flower year after year but may disappear underground during the winter. Then plant a range of bulbs that flower in spring, summer or fall to add pops of color to your landscaping. Foliage generally lasts longer than flowers, so include some shade-tolerant perennials with decorative leaves, such as hostas, arums, and pulmonarias—when combined, these will offer textural interest for many months. Once you have installed the permanent plants, fill the gaps with shade-loving annual bedding plants, which can also be used to brighten up pots on a patio.

The tobacco plant emits a sweet fragrance in the evening; plant it next to seating to enjoy the scent.

Red flowers such as these busy Lizzies look less bright in a shady position, and may look more yellow under full sun.

THE EFFECT OF LIGHT ON COLOR

We perceive some colors differently when viewing them in bright sunlight compared to deep shade. Some hues appear washed-out under sunny skies, while others that we think of as bright seem less luminous in shade. For example, at low light levels, blue and green foliage can appear brighter than red flowers, a phenomenon known as the Purkinje shift, and in brighter situations, reds look more yellow as the intensity of the sunlight increases (the Bezold-Brücke effect). It is therefore worth checking your color schemes in situ when matching plants.

FLOWERS AND FRAGRANCE

Many shade-adapted plants rely upon scent rather than color to lure pollinators such as bees and moths to their flowers. Such plants also typically produce small, white or pale-colored blooms that reflect light efficiently so they shine out from gloomy spots. While some of these flowers may not be as obviously glamorous as large, showy sun-lovers such as delphiniums and lupines, their quieter type of beauty is not to be underestimated and they can make an eye-catching feature when they are planted en masse. Aim for a succession of flowers and fragrant blooms, such as the sweet box (*Sarcococca*), lily-of-the-valley (*Convallaria*), osmanthus, tobacco plants (*Nicotiana*), and *Viburnum* × *bodnantense* 'Dawn', to stimulate the senses throughout the seasons.

INTRODUCING SEASONAL INTEREST

When planning your planting, aim for a sparkling show of color and interest to enjoy all year round. There is a wide choice of shade-lovers that perform at different times to make this dream a reality, but resist the urge to buy everything that's in bloom when you visit the nursery, which may fade soon after planting. Instead, make a chart with the 12 months of the year at the top, and list in each column the plants that pack a punch at that time to create a succession of beautiful flowers and foliage.

YEAR-ROUND COLOR

Creating beds that are packed with color all year round may be more challenging in a shady space than in a sunny one, but it is definitely achievable. Plan well ahead for all seasons and try not to be seduced by the flowers on display at garden centers and nurseries in spring and early summer, when the warmer weather generates an uptick in plant sales. Designed to tempt you into impromptu purchases, these plants will look spectacular for a few weeks, but then offer little to admire later in the year when past their prime.

Spread the interest by selecting plants recommended in this book that will deliver pops of color throughout the year, buying online if your local stores do not have those on your list—many online suppliers sell a wide range all year round, even when the plants do not look their best. You will then be pleasantly surprised when an unassuming clump of twigs planted in spring bursts forth with foliage and flowers as the seasons turn.

Make your beds and borders as large as possible, which will allow you to accommodate a wide selection of plants, including trees, shrubs, perennials, and bulbs, that together present a range of attractive qualities 365 days of the year.

Japanese maples offer year-round height and structure, while their flaming foliage creates a focal point in the fall.

SEASONAL PLANS

Planning for year-round color can be daunting if you are a novice gardener, but there are simple guidelines that may help. First, remember that foliage usually lasts longer than flowers, so choose plants for their leaf shape, texture, and color. A backdrop of shrubs and trees will pay dividends, with both evergreens and deciduous types providing height and structure all year. Perennials offer pops of color when in bloom, so choose early, mid-, and late season performers to keep the show going. Position them carefully to produce the best effects; most will start to die down as soon as flowering is over and the foliage will begin to look tattered, so place those that bloom later in the season toward the front of a border to disguise the waning early performers.

Hydrangeas may look dull in spring when you buy them, but they will explode with color later in the year.

DECIDUOUS VS EVERGREEN PLANTS

It's tempting to fill a space with evergreens for continuous leaf coverage, but this will deny you the joy of plants that offer glorious color at certain times of year. A good rule of thumb is to include a 1:3 ratio of evergreens to deciduous plants, bearing in mind that some of the latter may offer stem and flower interest through the winter. The paperbark maple (*Acer griseum*), twisted hazel (*Corylus avellana* 'Contorta'), and Cornelian cherry (*Cornus mas*) are good examples and all are suitable for small spaces (see pp.84–87).

Evergreen yew hedging creates a foil for the frosted seed heads of a *Miscanthus sinensis* grass in winter.

BULB BONANZAS

Many winter- and spring-flowering bulbs take advantage of the extra light beneath deciduous trees when their stems are bare. Bulbs are planted a full season before they bloom, so make a note to buy bags of daffodils, crocuses, anemones, scillas, and others in early fall. Dry bulbs represent great value for money, allowing you to create a sea of spring color for very little outlay. If congested roots beneath a tree make planting them difficult, try installing a shallow raised bed for your bulbs at least a yard (meter) away from the trunk. Look through those on pp.76–79 for ideas on what to plant where in your shady space.

Nodding daffodils beneath the boughs of a tree brighten up an early spring garden.

FRAGRANT PLEASURES

Including scented plants adds yet another sensory experience to a shady garden. Daphnes, witch hazels (*Hamamelis*), mahonias, and sweet box (*Sarcococca*) are just a few of the winter- and spring-flowering shade-lovers that will lift your spirits on cold days with their fragrance. Celebrate the seasons and welcome in your guests by placing them along pathways and close to the front door. In containers and small spaces, use lily of the valley (*Convallaria*), hyacinths, and narcissus to perfume the air.

Daphne odora lifts the spirits with its sweet perfume when the pink blooms open in early spring.

PLANTING FOR WILDLIFE

Research shows that a lack of biodiversity poses a major threat to our planet, reducing the number and range of pollinating insects that are vital for food production, while breaking down ecosystems that absorb carbon. Gardeners can play their part in reversing this trend by including as many different plants as possible to support a whole range of insects, birds, and other creatures that depend on them.

Crab apples support pollinators with blossom in spring, while birds and small mammals eat the fall fruits.

PLANTS FOR POLLINATORS

Bee, butterfly, and moth populations are on the decline worldwide owing to habitat loss, but our yards can help support these vital pollinating insects. Wild bees such as mason bees pollinate more plants than honeybees, and they are attracted to tree blossom and native shrubs and perennials. Crab apple (*Malus*), hawthorn (*Crataegus*), and rowan (*Sorbus*) trees will all attract a variety of bees, while shade-loving shrubs, such as daphnes, *Hydrangea paniculata*, rose of Sharon (*Hypericum calycinum*), mahonias, sweet box (*Sarcococca*), and viburnums are also favorites. Perennials and annuals with single flowers and easily accessible pollen and nectar draw in bees, too, so ensure that you include a selection of these valuable plants to boost their food supplies.

While butterflies are drawn to many sun-loving plants, they enjoy a palette of pollen-rich, shade-tolerant plants similar to that of bees and hoverflies. Good choices include the butterfly bush (*Buddleia*), Japanese anemones, blue wood asters (*Symphyotrichum cordifolium*), ivy, astrantias, hardy geraniums, and others with a "Plant for Pollinators" symbol on the label.

You can also cater for night-flying moths, which are often overlooked but play a key pollinating role—their caterpillars provide food for many baby birds in spring, too. Shade plants that support moth caterpillars include foxgloves (*Digitalis*), primulas, and fuchsias, while the adults like to feast on pale, night-scented blooms such as tobacco plants (*Nicotiana*) and honeysuckle (*Lonicera*). Leaving a patch of longer grass in wilder areas will help supplement moths' food sources and provide cover for other insects and wildlife.

Japanese anemones provide a source of pollen and nectar for many insects in late summer.

Birds flock to honesty in late summer, pecking at the papery cases to reach the large black seeds inside.

BRING IN THE BIRDS

Adult birds and their chicks eat a wide variety of berries and seeds, as well as insects and their larvae that feed on shade-loving plants. After the trees named opposite have fed pollinators in spring, they then provide a rich supply of fruits in the fall to nourish birds and other small creatures such as field mice and voles. Holly is another good choice for a wildlife-friendly yard, but remember to choose a female form that will produce the berries (see p.86).

Seed heads provide additional nutrients for birds, while many of the insects that sustain them over the winter months can be found hidden in deciduous plants' hollow stems and dried flowers as temperatures fall. Among the best seed-producing plants for shady places are annual honesty (*Lunaria annua*), hydrangeas, *Eupatorium*, and *Clematis tangutica*, which produces fluffy seed heads used by birds as nesting material.

Trees, dense shrubs, and prickly hedges also make excellent habitats for nesting birds and a whole host of animals and insects that use them for cover and food.

As fall arrives, the pink pollen-rich flowers of *Eupatorium* turn into seed heads loved by birds.

TOP TIP INCLUDE A WIDE RANGE OF POLLEN-RICH PLANTS AND THOSE THAT PRODUCE BERRIES AND SEEDS TO SPAN THE SEASONS SO THE WILDLIFE IN YOUR YARD IS NEVER SHORT OF SUPPLIES, EVEN IN THE DEPTHS OF WINTER.

MAKING A FLOWERBED

The best time to create a new bed or border is early fall or early spring, when the soil is moist and plants will establish quickly. Borderline hardy plants should be planted in spring, giving them a couple of seasons to put down roots before the cold winter weather sets in. Before carving out a new border, consider where it will be most effective and the size you require, then clear the site of weeds and prepare the soil to give your plants a good start in life.

SUITABLE SITES

When looking for a suitable location for a bed or border, check the light levels (see pp.22–23) and, if possible, make it large enough to include an area that receives a few hours of direct sun each day from spring to fall. It won't be a problem if none of the bed is in full sun (see p.13), but your planting options for part or dappled shade will be much broader than for areas in full shade that receive little or no direct light. A larger site will also allow you to accommodate a more diverse range of plants to celebrate seasonal changes and provide year-round interest (see pp.52–53).

In a large space, also consider the proximity of your water supply, since new plants will require extra irrigation while they are establishing, especially those under trees or close to a boundary where the soil will be particularly dry.

Mark out a new or extended rectangular border with string tied between two canes.

SHAPING UP

Squares, rectangles, circles, ovals, and sweeping curves generally look better than beds with irregular-shaped sides, which can look messy and are also more difficult to maintain if they are next to a lawn that needs edging.

Use string pulled taut between canes to mark out rectangular or square beds. To create a perfect circle, cut some string a little longer than the desired radius and tie it to a cane planted in the center. Then use the string with landscape paint like a compass to mark out the shape. The same technique can be used for a curved bed, or you can simply lay down a flexible hose to mark out a smooth outline.

Dig around the edges of the bed with a sharp spade, removing sods as you go, if you're cutting it out of a lawn. Place them upside down in a quiet corner to decompose; after a year, it will make a compost mulch for the bed.

Deep borders allow you to include a wide range of shade-tolerant plants that perform in different seasons.

IMPROVING THE SOIL

Leave the bed for a few weeks then weed it, digging out perennials and hoeing off annuals. If preparing it in the fall, lay cardboard over the soil and add a 2 in (5 cm) layer of organic matter such as well-rotted garden compost or a soil conditioner on top. This will block the light that weed seeds need to germinate, while gradually decomposing over winter to leave you with a clean bed ready for planting in spring. You can also do this in spring and plant the bed in the fall.

If you can't wait a season or two before planting, lay a thick mulch around your newly installed plants, taking care to leave gaps around the woody stems of trees and shrubs.

Remove all weeds from the bed and then add a mulch over a layer of cardboard.

DIVIDING PERENNIALS

Once established, many perennial plants will spread to form large clumps. Over time, the roots can become congested and the plant may then not flower well, but you can revitalize it and make new plants by dividing the clump. Carefully dig out the plant and then plunge a spade into the middle of the clump to divide it into two or more sections. Alternatively, use a pruning saw to cut through heavily congested root balls. Remove any dead parts and replant the newly divided sections with space for them to spread.

HOW TO PLANT SHRUBS, PERENNIALS, AND ANNUALS

This simple technique is suitable for most plants, apart from trees (see *pp.82–83*), and will help to ensure they establish well.

YOU WILL NEED Spade or trowel • plant • watering can or hose • mycorrhizal fungi (optional) • balanced organic feed such as bonemeal (optional)

1 Dig a hole twice as wide and about the same depth as the root ball—most plants should be planted at the same depth as they were in their pots.
2 Water the plant and then remove it from its pot. If the roots are twining round the edge of the root ball, gently tease them out before planting.
3 You can add some mycorrhizal fungi to the planting hole to encourage good root growth, but if you have chosen your plants carefully and they are suitable for your soil, you should not need to add fertilizer at this stage. However, if you think your soil is particularly infertile, add a balanced organic food such as bonemeal.

4 Place the plant in the hole, then refill around the roots with the excavated soil and gently press it down to remove any large air gaps. Using a hose on a fine spray or a watering can fitted with rose head, give the plant a long drink. Apply a mulch of compost or bark chips around the plants as described above. Water during dry spells until the roots are established.

SHADE-LOVING SHRUBS

Shrubs form the backbone of any yard. Whether evergreen or deciduous, these woody-stemmed plants provide essential height and structure throughout the year, and those listed here all thrive in shady spaces. By choosing a selection, you will be guaranteed an evolving show of foliage and flowers to brighten up gloomy areas throughout the year—but site them carefully, since they will be difficult to move once established. Before buying, also check that the shrubs you choose will suit your soil conditions (see *pp.24–25*).

MEXICAN ORANGE BLOSSOM *CHOISYA TERNATA*

HEIGHT AND SPREAD 8 x 8 ft (2.5 x 2.5 m)
SOIL Well-drained
HARDINESS Hardy to 14 to 5°F (−10 to −15°C)
SUN ☀ ◐

Many nurseries list this evergreen as a sun-lover but it copes well in shade, too, though the golden foliage of the cultivar SUNDANCE may lose its luster and revert to green in deep shade. In late spring, clusters of small, white, highly scented, star-shaped flowers appear in profusion among glossy, aromatic, dark green leaves. A sprinkling of blooms may also appear in summer. This handsome shrub is tolerant of most soils and easy to grow. Prune it after flowering if it outgrows its space.

Mexican orange blossom is covered in sweetly scented white flowers in late spring.

CAMELLIA *CAMELLIA* SPECIES

HEIGHT AND SPREAD Up to 10 x 6½ ft (3 x 2 m)
SOIL Moist but well-drained; acid
HARDINESS Hardy to 14 to 5°F (−10 to −15°C)
SUN ◐

These beautiful evergreen shrubs all enjoy part shade, and many flower in deeper shade, though they may bear fewer blooms. Their main flowering season is from midwinter to early spring, with blooms in colors ranging from white and pink to peach and dark red. Most are fairly hardy, but the petals may be damaged if sun thaws them rapidly after a frost, so avoid east-facing sites. They prefer a slightly acidic soil, but can be planted in a pot of acidic potting mix if you do not have the right conditions.

Camellias such as the pink-flowered 'Ave Maria' bring color in winter.

WINTER HAZEL *CORYLOPSIS PAUCIFLORA*

HEIGHT AND SPREAD 5 x 8 ft (1.5 x 2.5 m)
SOIL Moist but well-drained; acid
HARDINESS Fully hardy
SUN ◐

Grown for its pendent clusters of primrose-yellow flowers, which emit a wonderful scent when they appear on the bare stems in spring, this shrub also features rounded leaves that resemble those of a hazel tree. The foliage is bronze when young, then matures to bright green and turns orange-yellow in the fall before dropping. The winter hazel is ideal for an area at the edge of a tree canopy, preferring part shade and acid soil conditions. Prune it regularly after flowering to maintain an open framework of branches.

Winter hazel's scented, pale yellow flowers will lure you outdoors in spring.

DAPHNE *DAPHNE* SPECIES

HEIGHT AND SPREAD Up to 8 × 5 ft (2.5 × 1.5 m)
SOIL Moist but well-drained
HARDINESS Hardy to 5°F (−15°C)
SUN ☼ ◐ ☀

Of the *Daphne* genus, the most popular plants are evergreen shrubs suited to shady spots. The award-winning *D. bholua* 'Jacqueline Postill' produces deliciously scented pink flowers in winter when few other plants are in bloom, but needs a little sun to coax them to appear. For deeper shade, try the spurge laurel, *D. laureola*, which produces small, fragrant, yellow-green winter flowers, or *D. pontica*, with scented yellow spring flowers. Both form compact shrubs about 3 ft (1 m) high.

Daphne bholua 'Jacqueline Postill' is popular for its fragrant, pink-budded white flowers.

DEUTZIA *DEUTZIA × ELEGANTISSIMA*

HEIGHT AND SPREAD Up to 6½ × 5 ft (2 × 1.5 m)
SOIL Moist but well-drained
HARDINESS Hardy to 5°F (−15°C)
SUN ☼ ◐

This relatively compact deutzia is a deciduous shrub with small green leaves and clusters of pale pink, star-shaped flowers, borne in late spring and early summer. It is a good choice for brightening up a partly shaded area—if space is tight, you can opt for a smaller cultivar such as 'Rosalind', which is just under 3 ft (1 m) in height. Other deutzias, including *D. × hybrida* and *D. × rosea* and their cultivars, also cope with some shade. To prune, remove dead, diseased, and wayward stems after flowering.

In late spring, deutzias produce an abundance of pink, star-shaped flowers.

PAPERBUSH *EDGEWORTHIA PAPYRIFERA*

HEIGHT AND SPREAD Up to 5 × 5 ft (1.5 × 1.5 m)
SOIL Moist but well-drained
HARDINESS Hardy to 14°F (−10°C)
SUN ☼ ◐

In a sheltered or coastal yard, the paperbush makes a superb focal point for a semi-shaded area. In late winter, clusters of sweetly scented, tubular, yellow flowers appear on the bare stems of this unusual shrub, creating a striking display. Even before this, the silky flower buds, which look as if they're dusted with frost, make an eye-catching feature. Rarely succumbing to pests or diseases, the paperbush needs little pruning—just remove dead and wayward stems when you see them.

The unusual yellow flowers of the paperbush brighten up a shady yard in late winter.

OLEASTER *ELAEAGNUS × EBBINGEI*

HEIGHT AND SPREAD Up to 13 × 13 ft (4 × 4 m)
SOIL Moist but well-drained
HARDINESS Fully hardy
SUN ☼ ◐

This tough evergreen is also known as the silverberry due to the silvery sheen on the oval green leaves, which are also silver on the undersides. Popular cultivars include 'Gilt Edge', the foliage of which has golden edges, and 'Limelight', with yellow splashes on each leaf. In winter, the shrub bears tiny, cream, bell-shaped blooms with a sweet fragrance, followed by reddish berries. It makes a good hedging plant, providing year-round color and interest, although regular trimming may remove the flowers.

'Limelight' is a beautiful oleaster with dark green foliage with gold splashes.

JAPANESE ARALIA *FATSIA JAPONICA*

HEIGHT AND SPREAD Up to 10 × 10 ft (3 × 3 m)
SOIL Moist but well-drained
HARDINESS Hardy to 5°F (−15°C)
SUN ☼ ☼ ☀

Few shrubs can compete with the Japanese aralia for sculptural impact. This spreading evergreen bears dramatic hand-shaped, glossy green foliage, and in early fall spherical clusters of small white flowers appear, providing a feast for bees. They are followed by black berries, loved by birds. The cultivar 'Spider's Web' looks as if it is dusted with frost; 'Variegata' has cream-edged foliage. Japanese aralia is ideal for brightening up a border in deep shade, but will also be at home in a large pot.

The handsome foliage of the Japanese aralia will catch the eye in a shady border or large pot.

WITCH HAZEL *HAMAMELIS × INTERMEDIA*

HEIGHT AND SPREAD Up to 13 × 13 ft (4 × 4 m)
SOIL Well-drained; moist but well-drained
HARDINESS Hardy to 5°F (−15°C)
SUN ☼ ☼

Witch hazel's lightly scented red, orange, or yellow spidery flowers demand a closer look when they appear on the bare stems of this large deciduous shrub in the depths of winter. The oval green leaves form a muted backdrop to more colorful plants from spring to summer, after which they turn vibrant shades of orange and yellow in the fall before dropping. Happy in some shade, witch hazels grow best on slightly acid soils and need only a light prune in spring to keep them tidy.

'Jelena' produces lightly scented, coppery-orange flowers in winter.

SILK TASSEL BUSH *GARRYA ELLIPTICA*

HEIGHT AND SPREAD Up to 13 × 13 ft (4 × 4 m)
SOIL Well-drained
HARDINESS Hardy to 14°F (−10°C)
SUN ☼ ☼

This evergreen wall shrub is grown for its spectacular display of gray-green catkins, which appear in winter and can measure up to 8 in (20 cm). It also produces glossy, dark green foliage, felted gray beneath, while the popular cultivar 'James Roof' has wavy-edged leaves and silvery catkins. The shrub is dioecious, which means male and female flowers are on separate plants; the most spectacular catkins are on the males, while the females produce long clusters of purple-brown summer fruits.

The silk tassel bush gets its name from the catkins that cover the plant in winter.

HYDRANGEA *HYDRANGEA* SPECIES

HEIGHT AND SPREAD Up to 13 × 13 ft (4 × 4 m)
SOIL Moist but well-drained
HARDINESS Hardy to 5°F (−15°C)
SUN ☼ ☼

Three hydrangea species are particularly suited to shady yards—the mophead *H. macrophylla* (see also p.105), the snowball hydrangea, *H. arborescens*, and the shrubby *H. paniculata*—as well as hundreds of cultivars. Loved for their large flower heads, which appear in summer and fall, all hydrangeas thrive in light shade, but may not flower well in darker areas. They prefer moist soil, and the mopheads grow well in pots. When pruning, check the best method for your particular plant.

H. paniculata PINKY WINKY bears large, cone-shaped, white flower heads that fade to pink.

ROSE OF SHARON *HYPERICUM CALYCINUM*

HEIGHT AND SPREAD 2 × 3 ft (0.6 × 1 m)
SOIL Well-drained; moist but well-drained
HARDINESS Hardy to 5°F (−15°C)
SUN ☼ ☼ ☼

This spreading evergreen shrub is ideal for growing under trees and in the darkest areas of the yard, where it will cover the ground with dark green, oval leaves. The large, sunny yellow flowers bloom throughout summer and into fall, and are followed by red berries, which turn black in winter. The berried stems can be used in fall floral decorations for the home. Rose of Sharon requires little or no pruning, but you may need to dig out unwanted growth if it spreads too far.

Rose of Sharon will create leafy ground cover beneath trees, with the addition of golden flowers in summer.

MOUNTAIN LAUREL *KALMIA LATIFOLIA*

HEIGHT AND SPREAD Up to 3 × 3 ft (1 × 1 m)
SOIL Moist but well-drained; acid
HARDINESS Fully hardy
SUN ☼

The mountain laurel is a compact evergreen shrub with glossy, dark green foliage that provides a foil for other plants in a partly shaded bed. It also has its time in the limelight when large clusters of pink, bowl-shaped flowers open from eye-catching ribbed buds from late spring to early summer. They are available in various shades of pink, from deep burgundy to almost white, and there are also bicolored forms. Easy to grow, this shrub performs best in moist, acid soil and needs little pruning.

The pink blooms of this plant open from unusual ribbed buds in late spring.

SWITCH IVY *LEUCOTHOE*

HEIGHT AND SPREAD Up to 5 × 8 ft (1.5 × 2.5 m)
SOIL Moist but well-drained; acid
HARDINESS Fully hardy
SUN ☼ ☼

This evergreen shrub is grown primarily for its colorful foliage, which on popular cultivars such as SCARLETTA emerges dark maroon, turns green in summer, and then lights up the fall and winter yard with bronze and dark red tints. It can cope with deep shade, but the colors may be more subdued at lower light levels. Smaller cultivars make good ground cover on acid soils, or you can grow them in pots of acidic potting mix. Prune only to remove dead or diseased stems in late spring.

SCARLETTA is a popular form, its maroon young leaves turning dark red and bronze in the fall.

HIMALAYAN HONEYSUCKLE *LEYCESTERIA FORMOSA*

HEIGHT AND SPREAD Up to 8 × 8 ft (2.5 × 2.5 m)
SOIL Well-drained; moist but well-drained
HARDINESS Hardy to 5°F (−15°C)
SUN ☼ ☼

The tall, slightly arching hollow stems of this deciduous shrub feature pointed green leaves and pendent flower heads throughout summer and early fall. The blooms, which comprise small white flowers surrounded by purple bracts, sway in the breeze and create a beautiful focal point. When they fade they are replaced by dark purple berries. This suckering shrub will grow well in a partly shaded area and needs only a quick annual tidy-up in early spring to remove dead and diseased stems.

Himalayan honeysuckle's flower heads comprise small white flowers and purple bracts.

POOR MAN'S BOX *LONICERA NITIDA* 'BAGGESEN'S GOLD'

HEIGHT AND SPREAD Up to 5 × 5 ft (1.5 × 1.5 m)
SOIL Well-drained; moist but well-drained
HARDINESS Fully hardy
SUN ☼ ☼

Often used for hedging, this gold-leaved evergreen can also be grown as a single specimen. The foliage takes on a more green-yellow hue in the fall. If not trimmed regularly, it produces long, arching shoots and small, cream flowers in spring, followed by purple berries. Very undemanding, it grows in most soils. Cut back new growth hard in the first couple of years after planting to create a bushy framework; trim lightly in late spring and early fall after that if growing as a hedge.

The sprawling stems with golden leaves can be clipped to form a compact hedge.

WINTER HONEYSUCKLE

LONICERA × PURPUSII 'WINTER BEAUTY'

HEIGHT AND SPREAD Up to 8 × 8 ft (2.5 × 2.5 m)
SOIL Well-drained; moist but well-drained
HARDINESS Fully hardy
SUN ☼ ☼

This unassuming deciduous shrub makes a good foil for flowers from spring to early fall, coming into its own in winter when clusters of white, sweetly scented, tubular flowers appear on the bare branches. The flowers may then be followed by red berries as the foliage unfurls. Plant it where you can appreciate the fragrant blooms and prune established shrubs after flowering, removing about a third of the older shoots.

Highly scented white flowers appear on the bare branches of this large shrub in winter.

OREGON GRAPE *MAHONIA AQUIFOLIUM*

HEIGHT AND SPREAD Up to 3 × 5 ft (1 × 1.5 m)
SOIL Well-drained; moist but well-drained
HARDINESS Hardy to 5°F (−15°C)
SUN ☼ ☼

This useful evergreen will thrive in the shadiest areas of the yard, including under trees, its glossy green, slightly prickly leaves taking on purplish tints during winter and brightening up gloomy spots. In spring, large clusters of small, yellow flowers shine out of the dark and are followed by blue berries in summer. 'Apollo' is a popular cultivar that grows to just 2 ft (60 cm) in height. Other mahonias are also adapted to deep shade (see also *Mahonia × media, p.120*). Prune after flowering in early summer.

Golden-yellow flowers emerge in spring amid prickly foliage on this evergreen shrub.

OSMANTHUS *OSMANTHUS × BURKWOODII*

HEIGHT AND SPREAD Up to 10 × 10 ft (3 × 3 m)
SOIL Well-drained
HARDINESS Hardy to 5°F (−15°C)
SUN ☼ ☼

With its glossy, tooth-edged, dark green leaves, this evergreen shrub provides year-round interest in partly shaded areas. From mid- to late spring, the highly scented white flowers will welcome visitors to the yard if you plant your shrub at the entrance. While this osmanthus makes a sizable plant over time, it grows quite slowly and creates a beautiful feature in a large pot on a patio. It can also be grown as a hedge by trimming it once a year after flowering.

Pure white flowers cover this evergreen in spring, their perfume filling the air for weeks.

PORTUGAL LAUREL *PRUNUS LUSITANICA*

HEIGHT AND SPREAD Up to 40 × 40 ft (12 × 12 m)
SOIL Well-drained; moist but well-drained
HARDINESS Hardy to 5°F (−15°C)
SUN ☼ ☀

Not to be confused with cherry laurel (*Prunus laurocerasus*), which can be an invasive weed in the wild, Portugal laurel is better behaved and makes a beautiful evergreen hedge or specimen shrub. Its dark red shoots bear dark green, oval leaves, and when left untrimmed they are joined by long clusters of fragrant white flowers in early summer, followed by dark purple fruits. It also thrives on infertile soils. Prune in late spring, or later in summer if birds are nesting in it.

Ideal for hedging, Portugal laurel will create a leafy screen, with flowers in early summer.

FIRETHORN *PYRACANTHA*

HEIGHT AND SPREAD 8 × 8 ft (2.5 × 2.5 m)
SOIL Well-drained; moist but well-drained
HARDINESS Fully hardy
SUN ☼ ☀

This evergreen makes a superb hedge for a boundary, where its spiny stems will deter intruders. Firethorn also decorates the yard throughout the year with glossy, dark green foliage; sprays of white, early summer flowers; and bright orange, red, or yellow fall berries, which are its main attraction. While birds enjoy the fruits, these usually last well into winter. Firethorn is easy to grow; simply prune lightly in late winter or early spring, taking care not to remove all the flower buds.

Red-berried firethorns light up the yard in the fall and provide food for birds.

RHODODENDRON/AZALEA *RHODODENDRON*

HEIGHT AND SPREAD Up to 13 × 13 ft (4 × 4 m)
SOIL Moist but well-drained; acid
HARDINESS Fully hardy
SUN ☼ ☀

Choose a large evergreen rhododendron or smaller azalea (some of which are deciduous) to brighten up the yard with their colorful blooms from spring to early summer. The flowers of some are also fragrant. A few rhododendrons, especially *R. ponticum*, are classified as invasive, so ask at a reputable nursery for a well-behaved plant. Most rhododendrons require little pruning, except to remove dead or diseased stems after flowering.

'Percy Wiseman' is an evergreen shrub with pink-flushed spring blooms.

ROSE *ROSA*

HEIGHT AND SPREAD Up to 10 × 10 ft (3 × 3 m)
SOIL Moist but well-drained
HARDINESS Fully hardy
SUN ☼ ☀

While many roses like to bask in sun, a number grow well in part shade, as long as they're not near large trees or shrubs that will suck the moisture out of the soil. Wild roses, such as *Rosa rugosa* with its beautiful purple-pink flowers and large hips, thrive in some shade, while many modern cultivars also cope with low light conditions—search reputable rose nurseries online for their recommended shade-loving varieties. Pruning methods vary depending on the rose, so check online for the best way to cut yours back.

Rosa rugosa grows happily in some shade and produces colorful single blooms.

BUTCHER'S BROOM *RUSCUS ACULEATUS*

HEIGHT AND SPREAD 30 × 30 in (75 × 75 cm)
SOIL Well-drained; moist but well-drained
HARDINESS Hardy to 5°F (−15°C)
SUN ☼ ☼ ☼

This compact shrub loves shade and will even grow under tree canopies, where its lance-shaped, leaflike cladophylls (flattened stems) will create a colorful feature year-round. In spring, small, greenish flowers appear, followed on female plants by bright red berries in summer and fall. Because male and female flowers are on separate plants you may need both forms to guarantee berries; otherwise, look for hermaphrodite hybrids. It is very easy to grow—simply cut out dead stems in spring.

Butcher's broom produces red berries and flattened stems that resemble leaves.

SWEET BOX *SARCOCOCCA CONFUSA*

HEIGHT AND SPREAD Up to 6 × 3 ft (2 × 1 m)
SOIL Well-drained; moist but well-drained
HARDINESS Fully hardy
SUN ☼ ☼

Sweet box is a good choice for a dark corner of the yard, where for most of the year it will provide a leafy foil for shade-loving flowers. However, in the depths of winter, after the brighter blooms have died down, this compact evergreen puts on its annual show of small, spidery, white flowers, which have a sweet, vanilla-like scent. Growing well in dry shade, this shrub is a good choice for areas under trees, and it also copes with urban pollution. Prune lightly after it has flowered.

Sweet box's small winter flowers could be overlooked were it not for their scent.

SKIMMIA *SKIMMIA JAPONICA*

HEIGHT AND SPREAD Up to 3 × 3 ft (1 × 1 m)
SOIL Moist but well-drained
HARDINESS Fully hardy
SUN ☼ ☼

This slow-growing evergreen does well in shade, as long as the soil is consistently moist but not wet, which generally rules out areas below trees. Skimmias are dioecious (male and female flowers are borne on separate plants) and the male forms produce oval-shaped clusters of green or red winter buds followed by small, white or pink flowers. Female and hermaphrodite skimmias also produce berries (see p.109). All skimmias thrive in pots, and they require little or no pruning—just cut out dead or diseased growth.

'Rubella' is a male skimmia, with pink winter buds that open to pinkish-white flowers.

EARLY STACHYURUS *STACHYURUS PRAECOX*

HEIGHT AND SPREAD 8 × 8 ft (2.5 × 2.5 m)
SOIL Moist but well-drained; neutral to acid
HARDINESS Hardy to 5°F (−15°C)
SUN ☼ ☼

This large deciduous shrub produces slim, pointed, mid-green leaves that turn pink and yellow in the fall before dropping. While it makes a useful backdrop for other plants from spring to fall, it really shines during winter, when long clusters of bell-shaped, pale yellow flowers dangle from the bare stems; plant it where you will be able to see this spectacular show from the warmth of your house. Prune to remove dead or diseased growth in early spring.

Small yellow flowers held in pendant clusters appear on the early stachyurus in winter.

YEW *TAXUS BACCATA* 'STANDISHII'

HEIGHT AND SPREAD Up to 5 × 3 ft (1.5 × 1 m)
SOIL Well-drained
HARDINESS Fully hardy
SUN ☼ ☼ ☀

While all yews grow well in shade, this columnar evergreen is a good choice for small spaces, where it will brighten up a gloomy spot with its golden-yellow, needlelike foliage, although the color will be more subdued in deep shade. In the fall, it produces bright red berries, loved by birds. Use it to create a vertical accent in a border close to trees and other shrubs, or, if you prefer, clip it to form a tear-drop shape. Yews tolerate dry soil and need pruning only to remove dead and diseased wood.

The golden foliage of 'Standishii' is joined by bright red berries in the fall.

GUELDER ROSE *VIBURNUM OPULUS*

HEIGHT AND SPREAD 13 × 8 ft (4 × 2.5 m)
SOIL Well-drained; moist but well-drained
HARDINESS Fully hardy
SUN ☼ ☼ ☀

Grown for its large, maple-like, lobed leaves, which turn pink or red in fall, this large deciduous shrub produces flat-topped clusters of small, white flowers surrounded by larger sterile flowers in spring. These are followed by red berries; for yellow ones, seek out the cultivar 'Xanthocarpum'. It is a great plant for wildlife because the flowers attract pollinators and the berries are loved by birds. Plant it in a woodland setting or a dark, shady area of the yard. Prune after flowering in spring, if needed.

The lacy flower heads of the guelder rose are followed in the fall by bright red berries.

LAURUSTINUS *VIBURNUM TINUS*

HEIGHT AND SPREAD Up to 8 × 8 ft (2.5 × 2.5 m)
SOIL Well-drained; moist but well-drained
HARDINESS Hardy to 14°F (−10°C)
SUN ☼ ☼ ☀

This viburnum forms a large evergreen shrub with leathery, dark green leaves. From late winter, flat-topped clusters of deep pink buds open to reveal small, starry white flowers, which are followed in spring by metallic-blue berries. It is ideal as an evergreen hedge in coastal areas or yards where winter temperatures do not drop too low, or try it as a specimen in a mixed bed. It requires little pruning apart from the removal of dead, diseased, or wayward stems in spring after flowering.

Pink buds open to reveal tiny white flowers that persist for months on this decorative shrub.

WEIGELA *WEIGELA* 'FLORIDA VARIEGATA'

HEIGHT AND SPREAD 8 × 5 ft (2.5 × 1.5 m)
SOIL Well-drained
HARDINESS Fully hardy
SUN ☼ ☼

The annual show of funnel-shaped, pale pink flowers that appear in late spring and last for many weeks makes this easy-to-grow weigela a good choice for any partly shaded area of the yard. While the blooms are the main attraction, this beautiful deciduous shrub also sports decorative, cream-edged, gray-green leaves that keep the interest going from spring to fall. It tolerates dry soils and can be grown quite close to trees. Prune it in summer after flowering.

'Florida Variegata' is loved for its long-lasting pink spring flowers and decorative foliage.

SHADE-LOVING PERENNIALS

Many beautiful flowering perennials are adapted to life in the shade, and when combined, they can deliver a confection of colors from late winter through to the final days of fall. Select a range of plants that suit your conditions and bloom at different times of year, and also consider foliage interest, which will help sustain the show when they are not in flower. Set out each of your choices in groups of three or more to produce the most dramatic effect.

BEAR'S BREECHES *ACANTHUS SPINOSUS*

HEIGHT AND SPREAD Up to 5 × 3 ft (1.5 × 1 m)
SOIL Moist but well-drained
HARDINESS Fully hardy
SUN ☼ ☼

One of the best *Acanthus* species for a yard with dappled shade, this plant produces large, spiny-edged leaves and tall spikes of purple-hooded white flowers throughout the summer. Site it carefully, as it needs space for its sculptural foliage to spread and can be difficult to move once established. A good choice for a wild yard or the back of a border, bear's breeches will grow in most soils but may suffer from powdery mildew during dry summers. Lift and divide clumps in fall or spring.

The spiny leaves of bear's breeches create a sculptural feature below the large blooms.

MONK'S HOOD *ACONITUM CARMICHAELII*

HEIGHT AND SPREAD 5 ft × 20 in (1.5 × 0.5 m)
SOIL Moist but well-drained
HARDINESS Fully hardy
SUN ☼ ☼

Ideal for a partly shaded border where the soil does not dry out too much, this tall perennial with divided green foliage can easily go unnoticed for most of the summer as other flowers come and go. Then, just as much of the yard is looking tired, spikes of deep blue, hooded flowers appear, creating a focal point from late summer to mid-fall. As they are highly poisonous, these plants are not a good choice for yards used by young children or pets. Wear gloves when handling them.

'Kelmscott' flowers in the fall, when spikes of large, lavender-blue blooms appear.

BUGBANE *ACTAEA SIMPLEX*

HEIGHT AND SPREAD Up to 4 × 2 ft (1.2 × 0.6 m)
SOIL Moist but well-drained; neutral to acid
HARDINESS Fully hardy
SUN ☼

Bugbane makes its mark in the fall when bottlebrush-shaped, pinkish-white flowers appear above the deeply divided foliage. The most popular cultivars, including those in the Atropurpurea Group, have dark purple leaves, adding extra interest earlier in the season. While this perennial enjoys shade, it prefers moist soil, so avoid areas under trees or close to walls, where conditions will be too dry. The seed heads are a beautiful winter feature; remove them in spring to make way for new growth.

Dark foliage combined with pinkish-white flowers adds impact to a fall yard.

EASTERN BLUESTAR *AMSONIA TABERNAEMONTANA*

HEIGHT AND SPREAD Up to 24 × 20 in (60 × 50 cm)
SOIL Moist but well-drained
HARDINESS Hardy to 5°F (−15°C)
SUN ☼ ☀

Grown for its clusters of starry, sky-blue flowers, this clump-forming perennial will be happy in lightly shaded areas of the yard. The blooms appear from late spring to midsummer and are held on upright stems of lance-shaped foliage, which turns yellow in the fall. The attractive seed heads can be left on the plants to decorate the winter yard. Plant this elegant perennial toward the front of a border or in another site where the flowers can be clearly seen. Cut down the old stems in spring.

The sky-blue flowers of the eastern bluestar combine well with pink and white blooms.

JAPANESE ANEMONE *ANEMONE × HYBRIDA*

HEIGHT AND SPREAD 4 ft × 20 in (1.2 × 0.5 m)
SOIL Well-drained; moist but well-drained
HARDINESS Fully hardy
SUN ☼ ☀

Decorating the yard in late summer with their saucer-shaped flowers, Japanese anemones thrive in dappled shade close to trees and large shrubs. The blooms, in white or many shades of pink, are held on sturdy stems above large, green, lobed leaves. *A. × hybrida* is less likely to spread than *A. hupehensis* (see p.118), which is best kept to wilder areas of the yard where it can multiply freely. As well as giving late-season color, the flowers of this hardy perennial are loved by pollinators.

'Luise Uhink' is a white cultivar that blooms over a long period from late summer.

COLUMBINE *AQUILEGIA*

HEIGHT AND SPREAD Up to 39 × 20 in (1 × 0.5 m)
SOIL Moist but well-drained
HARDINESS Fully hardy
SUN ☼ ☀

Offering a wide range of colors, these cottage-garden favorites bloom from late spring to early summer. *A. vulgaris* is known as granny's bonnet, since the flowers look like little hats, while other species have petals with dramatic spurs. The blooms appear over fernlike foliage and offer a nectar-rich feast for bees. All are easy to grow and will self-seed, the offspring often bearing traits from both plant parents if more than one species or color is grown. They may succumb to mildew on dry, free-draining soil.

'Black Barlow' is a prized cultivar bearing dark maroon flowers with yellow eyes.

ITALIAN ARUM *ARUM ITALICUM*

HEIGHT AND SPREAD 14 × 20 in (35 × 50 cm)
SOIL Well-drained
HARDINESS Fully hardy
SUN ☼ ☀

The most commonly grown Italian arum is the cultivar 'Marmoratum', which features arrow-shaped, glossy green foliage with distinctive white patterns. It appears in late fall and overwinters, shining bright on gloomy days, then dies back in summer, just as spikes of greenish-yellow blooms appear. These are followed by orange berries, which add a splash of color to the yard in early fall. All parts are poisonous, so do not plant in yards used by young children or pets; wear gloves when handling.

'Marmoratum' is grown for its patterned winter foliage as well as the bright orange berries.

FALSE GOATSBEARD *ASTILBE*

HEIGHT AND SPREAD Up to 24 × 18 in (60 × 45 cm)
SOIL Moist; moist but well-drained
HARDINESS Fully hardy
SUN ☀

The perfect plant for a shady area close to a pond or in a bog garden, the moisture-loving false goatsbeard bears feather-like flower heads in red, pink, or white throughout the summer. The seed heads provide winter interest if left in situ. This pretty perennial is also grown for its attractive divided foliage, which appears before the flowers, and often has bronze tints when young. All species and cultivars prefer moist soil and do not tolerate dry, sandy conditions. Divide large clumps in late winter or early spring.

Astilbes are perfect for pondside locations, where they will thrive in the damp soil.

ASTRANTIA *ASTRANTIA*

HEIGHT AND SPREAD Up to 36 × 18 in (90 × 45 cm)
SOIL Moist but well-drained
HARDINESS Fully hardy
SUN ☀ ☀

Resembling little pincushions, the dainty flowers of these cottage-garden perennials appear in early summer and bloom over a long period. Available in shades of pink, maroon, or greenish-white, they are held over lobed green foliage. While they prefer moist, well-drained soil, these plants are fairly easy-going and will perform well in drier conditions, but may not flower as profusely if grown in deep shade. They die back in the fall and reappear in spring, requiring almost no maintenance.

'Buckland' bears a profusion of large, pale pink flowers with green tints in early summer.

ELEPHANT'S EARS *BERGENIA*

HEIGHT AND SPREAD 20 × 20 in (50 × 50 cm)
SOIL Moist but well-drained
HARDINESS Hardy to 5°F (−15°C)
SUN ☀ ☀ ☀

Named after their large, leathery, evergreen leaves, these shade-loving perennials can be grown under trees and large shrubs, where their foliage will create a beautiful textural carpet. The leaves often take on red tints in winter; in some cultivars they are purple-bronze with pink undersides all year round. Spikes of small pink or white flowers, loved by pollinators, appear in spring. Remove old foliage in spring as new growth appears and take off faded flower heads in early summer, after the plants have bloomed.

Bergenias offer a carpet of large, glossy, evergreen foliage and colorful flowers in spring.

BISTORT *BISTORTA*

HEIGHT AND SPREAD Up to 32 × 20 in (80 × 50 cm)
SOIL Moist but well-drained
HARDINESS Fully hardy
SUN ☀ ☀

You may find these spreading perennials listed under their former name of *Persicaria*. Most flower well in part shade; the best for gardens include the tall *B. amplexicaulis*, which produces wands of pink or red flowers in summer over spear-shaped foliage, and the shorter *B. affinis*, commonly known as lesser knotweed, which grows to 10 in (25 cm) high. The latter makes good ground cover and has oval foliage with shorter spikes of pink or white blooms. Both prefer moist soil, so avoid dry areas under trees.

Bright red or pink flower spikes appear over spear-shaped foliage in late summer.

SIBERIAN BUGLOSS *BRUNNERA MACROPHYLLA*

HEIGHT AND SPREAD 20 × 20 in (50 × 50 cm)
SOIL Moist but well-drained
HARDINESS Fully hardy
SUN ☼ ☼

The Siberian bugloss is a good choice for areas of the yard that rarely dry out completely. Thriving in deep shade, it produces rough-textured, heart-shaped leaves that cover the soil and, in spring, clusters of mauve-blue flowers that resemble forget-me-nots. Popular cultivars include 'Dawson's White', with cream-edged foliage, and 'Jack Frost', the leaves of which feature silvery patterns. These perennials are easy to grow, though the young foliage may be nibbled by slugs and snails.

'Dawson's White' sports green leaves with cream margins and mauve-blue flowers.

SEDGE *CAREX*

HEIGHT AND SPREAD Up to 24 × 24 in (60 × 60 cm)
SOIL Well-drained; moist but well-drained
HARDINESS Fully hardy
SUN ☼ ☼

While most grasses prefer a sunny site, sedges are more adaptable and can be grown in some shade. Opt for plain green or stripy-leaved types, such as *C. oshimensis* 'Evergold' and *C. morrowii* 'Everglow', which will cover the ground with fountains of colorful evergreen leaves. These grasslike plants tolerate dry soils, and while they may lose a little color in deep shade, they will still offer textural interest in gloomier areas. Bowles's golden sedge, *Carex elata* 'Aurea', is a good choice for damp soils.

Sedges are perfect for cool, shady spots, where they will create foliage interest.

TWISTED SHELL FLOWER *CHELONE OBLIQUA*

HEIGHT AND SPREAD 24 × 24 in (60 × 60 cm)
SOIL Moist but well-drained; moist
HARDINESS Hardy to 5°F (−15°C)
SUN ☼ ☼

Also known as turtlehead, a reference to the shape of its unusual deep pink or purple flowers, this decorative perennial also features veined and tooth-edged green foliage. The flowers appear over a long period from late summer to mid-fall. This plant thrives in moist soil and can be grown in a bog garden or a shady area close to a pond or stream. Applying a deep mulch in spring will help the soil retain moisture during the summer months. Lift and divide large clumps in spring or fall.

Given moist soil, the twisted shell flower will reward you with a profusion of pink blooms.

BARRENWORT *EPIMEDIUM*

HEIGHT AND SPREAD Up to 24 × 24 in (60 × 60 cm)
SOIL Well-drained; moist but well-drained
HARDINESS Fully hardy
SUN ☼ ☼

These semi-evergreen or evergreen perennials are perfect for gloomy areas, most coping with the deep shade and dry soil beneath trees. Grown primarily for their heart-shaped leaves, which may have red or bronze tints, they create a beautiful textured ground cover. In spring, small, spidery flowers in colors ranging from yellow and orange to pink and purple appear on wiry stems. Cut back old and tattered foliage just before the flower stems appear in early spring.

Epimediums produce colorful foliage accompanied by spidery flowers in spring.

CRANESBILL _GERANIUM_

HEIGHT AND SPREAD Up to 32 × 24 in (80 × 60 cm)
SOIL Well-drained; moist but well-drained
HARDINESS Fully hardy
SUN ☼ ☼

Cranesbills, or hardy geraniums, are happy in moist soils and light shade, though some will tolerate darker spots, too. These easy-to-grow perennials with lobed foliage produce flowers in shades of purple, pink, blue, and white from late spring to midsummer—deadhead them to prolong the display. Avoid the alpine types such as those in the Cinereum Group, which need full sun to bloom. Cranesbills usually disappear in winter, though a few may retain some foliage year-round.

ROZANNE is loved for its bright blue flowers with pale centers that bloom throughout summer.

HELLEBORE _HELLEBORUS_

HEIGHT AND SPREAD Up to 24 × 24 in (60 × 60 cm)
SOIL Moist but well-drained
HARDINESS Fully hardy
SUN ☼

These perennials are the mainstay of a winter garden, their nodding heads of white, green, pink, or purple flowers appearing from midwinter and often lasting well into spring. The Oriental hybrids (_Helleborus_ × _hybridus_) are fully hardy, but the flowers of the Christmas rose, _H. niger_, and those of _H. lividus_ and _H. thibetanus_ may be damaged by cold, wet weather, so grow them in a sheltered spot. Remove old leaves as the flowering stems appear to keep plants neat and prevent the spread of diseases.

'Anna's Red' is a beautiful long-flowering hellebore with marbled evergreen foliage.

BLEEDING HEART _LAMPROCAPNOS SPECTABILIS_

HEIGHT AND SPREAD Up to 32 × 32 in (80 × 80 cm)
SOIL Moist but well-drained
HARDINESS Fully hardy
SUN ☼ ☼

Formerly known as _Dicentra spectabilis_, bleeding heart is an elegant shade-lover that produces arching stems of heart-shaped flowers from mid- to late spring. The pink and white blooms create an eye-catching focal point, while the bright green, ferny foliage adds another beautiful feature. Ideally, grow bleeding heart in moist soil, although it will tolerate drier conditions. As the whole plant dies down in the summer, remember where you have planted it to avoid digging it up. Apply an organic mulch in spring.

The heart-shaped pink-and-white flowers give this plant its common name.

FALSE SOLOMON'S SEAL _MAIANTHEMUM RACEMOSUM_

HEIGHT AND SPREAD 30 × 20 in (75 × 50 cm)
SOIL Moist but well-drained; neutral to acid
HARDINESS Fully hardy
SUN ☼ ☼

You may find this beautiful woodland plant with its green, deeply veined, oval foliage under its former name of _Smilacina racemosa_. In late spring, cone-shaped clusters of small, fluffy, creamy-white flowers with a sweet scent appear at the tips of the arching leafy stems. These are sometimes followed by red fruits in late summer or early fall. Site it close to a pathway or seating area where you can enjoy the fragrance. Mulching each spring helps create the humus-rich conditions it enjoys.

Cone-shaped clusters of scented flowers bloom in spring on this shade-loving woodlander.

CAPPADOCIAN NAVELWORT

OMPHALODES CAPPADOCICA

HEIGHT AND SPREAD 10 × 8 in (25 × 20 cm)
SOIL Moist but well-drained; moist
HARDINESS Hardy to 5°F (–15°C)
SUN ☼

This diminutive clump-forming perennial is ideal for areas close to trees and shrubs, where its hairy, evergreen foliage will form a carpet over the soil. Loose clusters of bright blue flowers with white eyes appear over the foliage in spring—the blooms of the cultivar 'Cherry Ingram' are slightly larger than those of the species. Navelwort is generally easy to grow if your soil retains moisture through the summer. Divide clumps in early spring.

'Cherry Ingram' is a popular cultivar with pink-budded, dainty little blue flowers in spring.

PENSTEMON *PENSTEMON*

HEIGHT AND SPREAD Up to 32 × 24 in (80 × 60 cm)
SOIL Well-drained
HARDINESS Hardy to 23°F (–5°C)
SUN ☼ ☼

Loved for their tall stems of trumpet-shaped blooms and long flowering season, penstemons come in an array of colors, including white, red, and purple, with many sporting bi-colored blooms. Deadhead them regularly. These perennials tolerate only light shade and may not flower in darker spots, and they also need free-draining soil to thrive. Good drainage will also help them survive lower temperatures in winter. If you live in a cold area, pot up plants and place them in a sheltered spot over winter.

'Alice Hindley' produces tall stems of pale mauve flowers throughout summer.

PERENNIAL PHLOX *PHLOX PANICULATA*

HEIGHT AND SPREAD Up to 39 × 20 in (1 × 0.5 m)
SOIL Moist but well-drained
HARDINESS Fully hardy
SUN ☼ ☼

Border or perennial phlox are grown for their clusters of small, sweetly scented flowers, which appear from late summer to early fall. Their colors range from pure white to pink, red, and purple, with some in two shades, and they appear on stems covered with small lance-shaped green leaves. These plants will be happy in light shade but will not bloom in darker areas close to trees, where the dry soil may not suit them either. Mulch annually and divide large clumps in fall or spring.

'Peacock Cherry Red' will brighten up a shady spot with its vibrant blooms.

JACOB'S LADDER *POLEMONIUM CAERULEUM*

HEIGHT AND SPREAD 32 × 12 in (80 × 30 cm)
SOIL Moist but well-drained
HARDINESS Fully hardy
SUN ☼ ☼

This delicate-looking perennial is named after its leaves, which develop in opposite pairs said to resemble little ladders climbing the stems. In early summer, clusters of bell-shaped, lavender-blue flowers with orange or yellow stamens appear on tall stems above the foliage; cutting back the stems can encourage a second flush of blooms later in the season. This plant is short-lived but, where happy, it will self-seed. It requires little maintenance once established, apart from a mulch in spring.

Jacob's ladder decorates in early summer with its sprays of lavender blue flowers.

SOLOMON'S SEAL *POLYGONATUM × HYBRIDUM*

HEIGHT AND SPREAD Up to 36 × 24 in (90 × 30 cm)
SOIL Moist but well-drained
HARDINESS Fully hardy
SUN ☀

Graceful arching stems of green leaves with deep veins create a beautiful feature in a cool, shady spot when this perennial emerges in spring. Green-tipped white flowers that hang from the stems like little bells appear a few weeks later, followed by black fruits—though you may never see the latter if Solomon's seal sawfly caterpillars get to your plants first. While they often defoliate plants after they have bloomed, they do no long-lasting damage and your Solomon's seals will pop up the following year as usual.

Green-tipped white flowers hang gracefully from arching stems in early summer.

PRIMROSE *PRIMULA*

HEIGHT AND SPREAD Up to 18 × 12 in (45 × 30 cm)
SOIL Moist but well-drained; moist
HARDINESS Fully hardy
SUN ☀

Most primroses thrive in a cool spot in part shade, and there is a wide variety for different areas of the yard. *P. vulgaris*, with its pale yellow trumpet-shaped flowers, will flower well in fertile soil at the front of a border. The choices for damp soils include *P. vialii*, with rocket-shaped flower spikes made up of small purple blooms that open from red buds, and the candelabra primulas, such as *P. sieboldii* and *P. bulleyana*, which produce clusters of colorful flowers that appear at intervals up the stems.

Candelabra primulas come in a range of colors and prefer a shady site with damp soil.

LUNGWORT *PULMONARIA RUBRA*

HEIGHT AND SPREAD Up to 12 × 12 in (30 × 30 cm)
SOIL Well-drained; moist but well-drained
HARDINESS Fully hardy
SUN ☀ ☀

These ground-hugging plants produce a semi-evergreen carpet of hairy green leaves, many with white splashes, and small blue, pink, or white blooms in spring. Some cultivars, including 'Raspberry Splash' and 'Silver Bouquet', bear pink flowers that fade to blue, giving a duo-tone effect. Lungwort is not picky about soil type and will soon spread to fill a gap in a shady border. After flowering, remove any leaves suffering from powdery mildew and water the plants; the fresh new growth should be disease-free.

'Raspberry Splash' produces pink flowers that fade to blue, lending a two-tone effect.

FEATHERLEAF RODGERSIA *RODGERSIA PINNATA*

HEIGHT AND SPREAD Up to 4 × 4 ft (1.2 × 1.2 m)
SOIL Moist but well-drained; moist
HARDINESS Fully hardy
SUN ☀ ☀ ☀

A striking architectural plant, this rodgersia has divided, textured leaves that have a bronze tone, turning coppery-brown in the fall. Sturdy stems topped with clusters of fluffy-looking flowers, which come in white, cream, pink, or red, rise above the foliage in summer. They last for many weeks and are followed in the fall by claret-colored seed heads that persist through winter, deepening in color as the season progresses. Rodgersias need moisture as well as shade, so do not plant them too close to trees.

Rodgersias are grown for their large, sculptural foliage as well as the summer flowers.

BLUE WOOD ASTER *SYMPHYOTRICHUM CORDIFOLIUM*

HEIGHT AND SPREAD Up to 4 × 2 ft (1.2 × 0.6 m)
SOIL Moist but well-drained
HARDINESS Fully hardy
SUN ☼ ◑

Many asters thrive in sunny sites, but the blue wood aster and a few others are adapted to shady woodland edges. This tall species has small, heart-shaped, dark green leaves and, in late summer, a cloud of little mauve-blue, starry flowers on tall slim stems. One of the most popular hybrids is 'Little Carlow', which produces masses of violet-blue flowers. The stems may need staking, and while this aster grows on most soils, it prefers some moisture and will appreciate a mulch applied each spring.

'Little Carlow' is a popular cultivar, loved by pollinators for its nectar-rich flowers.

FRINGE CUPS *TELLIMA GRANDIFLORA*

HEIGHT AND SPREAD 32 × 12 in (80 × 30 cm)
SOIL Well-drained; moist but well-drained
HARDINESS Hardy to 14°F (−10°C)
SUN ◑

A perfect choice for areas of dry shade close to trees, this woodland plant offers a long season of interest. Its tall stems of small, bell-shaped, cream flowers appear in late spring and bloom until midsummer above rosettes of scalloped green leaves. Remove the flower stems after they have faded and plant later-flowering perennials in front to disguise the dying foliage. Divide clumps in spring and apply a mulch at the same time to help conserve soil moisture and improve its structure.

Fringe cups will dress up a border with its scallop-edged leaves and wands of blooms.

MEADOW RUE *THALICTRUM*

HEIGHT AND SPREAD Up to 39 × 18 in (100 × 45 cm)
SOIL Moist but well-drained
HARDINESS Fully hardy
SUN ◑

The most popular meadow rues are *T. aquilegiifolium*, which produces clusters of fluffy mauve or white flowers in summer, and *T. delavayi*, with tiny bell-shaped blooms. Both hold the flowers on tall stems above ferny foliage and have an airy quality, allowing you to see through to other plants behind. They like moist conditions, so mulch each spring to reduce evaporation rates and improve the soil structure. Use ring or brushwood supports to hold up the delicate stems when they are laden with flowers.

Thalictrum delavayi produces sprays of dainty mauve flowers on wiry stems in summer.

BELLWORT *UVULARIA GRANDIFLORA*

HEIGHT AND SPREAD Up to 18 × 18 in (45 × 45 cm)
SOIL Well-drained; moist but well-drained
HARDINESS Fully hardy
SUN ☼ ☀

An elegant woodland plant that will colonize areas close to trees, bellwort produces slightly drooping foliage and large yellow flowers that hang from the stems like golden earrings from late spring, the petals often slightly twisted at the tips. They are a magnet for pollinators such as bees. While not too picky about the soil, bellwort prefers some moisture and will thrive if you apply a mulch around it each year in spring. This plant will die down after it has bloomed.

Bellwort's drooping leaves and pendent flowers create a stunning combination.

PLANTING SHADE-LOVING BULBS

Spring bulbs provide pops of color in a shady yard just when they are needed most. Snowdrops, daffodils, grape hyacinths, crocuses, anemones, and others will bloom beneath deciduous trees and shrubs, making the most of the spring sun filtering through their bare canopies. Include summer- and fall-flowering bulbs, too, so the colorful show will continue after these early bloomers have faded.

Plant hyacinth bulbs in pots in the fall for a colorful, scented patio display the following spring.

Anemones grow from little corms that look like twigs and are planted just beneath the soil surface in the fall.

PLANTING SPRING BULBS

Most bulbs that flower in spring are planted in the fall, and you will notice garden centers stocked with a host of daffodils, grape hyacinths (*Muscari*), anemones, and hyacinths beginning in late summer.

Some plants that are grouped under "bulbs" actually grow from corms or tubers, which look slightly different from what you may be expecting. For example, the corms of *Anemone blanda* resemble little sticks, while winter aconites (*Eranthis hyemalis*) grow from small round tubers.

When planting spring bulbs, dig a hole about three times the depth of the bulb and plant them in groups, spaced at the intervals recommended on the packaging, with the pointed end facing up. Then simply cover them with soil and wait until spring. If you have squirrels in the yard, protect your bulbs from being eaten by placing chicken wire over the planting area, securing it with heavy stones or bricks; remove it as soon as shoots appear.

Anemone blanda corms are planted just below the surface, while winter aconite and cyclamen tubers should be planted at a depth of 1¼–2 in (3–5 cm), with the flat or hollow area facing up.

Buy your snowdrops in leaf, known as "in the green," in spring to guarantee a good show the following winter.

BULBS "IN THE GREEN"

Some bulbs dry out quickly and are more difficult to establish in the fall. These include snowdrops (*Galanthus*), bluebells (*Hyacinthoides non-scripta*), and lily of the valley (*Convallaria majalis*),

which are sold "in the green." This simply means they will be delivered to you just after flowering in spring, with fresh stems and leaves attached to the bulbs. You then plant them so the bulb and white area of the stem is buried beneath the soil surface.

DIVIDING CONGESTED BULBS

If your spring bulbs are not putting on their usual performance, they may be congested and will need to be divided. Wait until the flowers have faded and the foliage has started to wither, then dig up the clump. Carefully prise apart the congested bulbs, discarding any that are rotten or look diseased, and replant in smaller groups.

Dig up and divide congested clumps of bulbs after the flowers have faded in late spring or early summer.

Plant begonia tubers in trays of peat-free potting mix indoors in spring, with the hollow sides facing up.

ADDING SUMMER BULBS

Shade-loving bulbs that bloom in the summer and fall, including begonias, martagon lilies, and ivy-leaved cyclamen (*Cyclamen hederifolium*), are planted in spring. These beautiful plants will offer many months of color when grown in combination in a partly shady area. Cyclamen tubers can be planted directly outside in the ground, about 1¼–2 in (3–5 cm) deep—do not bury them too deeply or they may not flower. Plant lily bulbs in the ground or in containers with the flat area, which may have some roots growing from it, facing down, at a depth of about two-and-a-half times the height of the bulb.

Begonias are not frost-hardy and the tubers should be planted indoors in early spring. Fill a pot or seed tray with

moist seed starting mix about 3 in (7.5 cm) deep. Place the tubers on the surface with the hollow side facing up and about ¾ in (2 cm) apart, then cover with a further 1 in (2.5 cm) of seed mix. When leaves emerge, transplant them to individual pots of peat-free potting mix. Harden off the plants about two weeks before the last frosts in late spring by placing the pots outside during the day and bringing them in again at night. This helps acclimatize them to the lower temperatures. Use your begonias to decorate shady beds and pots with a continuous show of flowers. Bring them in before the first frosts.

TOP TIP MARK THE AREAS WHERE YOU HAVE PLANTED SPRING BULBS SO YOU DO NOT INADVERTENTLY DIG THEM UP WHEN THEY ARE DORMANT IN SUMMER.

SHADE-LOVING BULBS

Providing a succession of colors for many months of the year, shade-loving bulbs brighten gloomy spaces where few other plants will thrive and some even flower in winter when little else is in bloom. Bags of dry bulbs are also a great value, costing relatively little compared to the price of fully grown plants. Try the selection here for a garden filled with beautiful blooms, and use the guide on pp.74–75 to discover how and when to plant the different types.

WOOD ANEMONE *ANEMONE BLANDA*

HEIGHT AND SPREAD 6 × 6 in (15 × 15 cm)
SOIL Well-drained
HARDINESS Fully hardy
SUN ☼ ☼

The daisylike blue, mauve, pink, or white flowers of this little plant appear above ferny foliage in early spring, carpeting the ground beneath deciduous trees before their leaves unfurl. Wood anemones grow from twiglike corms that are planted in the fall, or you can buy the flowers in pots in spring. Where happy, plants soon spread into large clumps. Planting close to trees and shrubs reduces the soil moisture levels in winter, which helps prevent the corms from rotting.

'Violet Star' produces rich mauve flowers with white eyes and contrasting yellow stamens.

BEDDING BEGONIA *BEGONIA*

HEIGHT AND SPREAD Up to 20 × 12 in (50 × 30 cm)
SOIL Well-drained
HARDINESS Hardy to 32°F (0°C)
SUN ☼ ☼

Tuberous begonias offer a wealth of flower shapes and colors to decorate beds and containers from early summer to the first frosts. Many have beautiful foliage and offer a long season of interest for partly shaded areas. Plant tubers in spring (see p.74) or buy young plants and plant out after all risk of frost has passed. Good choices include the Million Kisses range, with flowers in many colors and distinctive angel-winged leaves, and the Illumination Series, with their trailing stems of small, bright blooms.

The Million Kisses range of begonias offers trailing stems of colourful flowers.

GIANT HIMALAYAN LILY *CARDIOCRINUM GIGANTEUM*

HEIGHT AND SPREAD Up to 10 × 1 ft (3 × 0.3 m)
SOIL Moist but well-drained
HARDINESS Fully hardy
SUN ☼

Few plants can match the giant Himalayan lily for sheer impact, its towering stems of large, scented, lily-shaped, white flowers with maroon throats appearing over bronze-tinted green leaves in summer. Look for flower-ready bulbs, which are planted just below the soil surface in the fall, or you may have to wait a few years for blooms to appear. This bulb dies after flowering, but produces new bulbs and seedlings that will spring up around the old plant to replace it. Top-dress in winter with leaf mold or a deep mulch.

The lily's large, scented flowers held on towering stems demand attention in a shady space.

LILY OF THE VALLEY *CONVALLARIA MAJALIS*

HEIGHT AND SPREAD 10 × 12 in (25 × 30 cm)
SOIL Moist but well-drained; poorly drained
HARDINESS Fully hardy
SUN ☼ ☼

Perfect for a spot at the edge of a tree canopy or in the shade of a wall, the much-loved lily of the valley delivers its sweet-scented, bell-shaped blooms in late spring. The stems of dainty flowers appear among spear-shaped green leaves. While it has a preference for moist soil, it will grow in drier conditions, where an annual application of leaf mold will help keep it happy. The tubers, known as pips, are available in the fall, but plants are usually sold as rooted crowns "in the green" in spring (see p.75).

The white flowers of 'Hardwick Hall' join cream-edged leaves in late spring.

CROCUS *CROCUS*

HEIGHT AND SPREAD 4 × 2 in (10 × 5 cm)
SOIL Well-drained
HARDINESS Fully hardy
SUN ☼ ☼

The goblet-shaped flowers of crocuses are ideal for lighting up lawns and areas beneath trees and shrubs. The colors range from golden-yellow and white to purple and pink, with some cultivars featuring striped or bicolored petals. While most species appear in late winter or early spring, the Byzantine crocus, *Crocus banaticus*, flowers in early fall and prefers damp soil. All are loved by pollinators and are particularly valuable to bumblebees. Plant the little corms in the fall for spring or fall flowers.

The violet flowers of *Crocus tommasinianus* often bloom in late winter.

IVY-LEAVED CYCLAMEN *CYCLAMEN HEDERIFOLIUM*

HEIGHT AND SPREAD 4 × 4 in (10 × 10 cm)
SOIL Well-drained
HARDINESS Hardy to 5°F (−15°C)
SUN ☼

Providing sparkling blooms in shady areas during the fall, this beautiful cyclamen has pink flowers with swept-back petals that appear before or at the same time as the leaves push through the soil. Grown for the eye-catching foliage as much as the flowers, this little plant has ivy-shaped leaves decorated with silvery and pale green patterns that offer interest long after the blooms have faded. The plant then goes dormant from late spring through midsummer. Plant the tubers in spring or buy plants in pots.

The marbled, ivy-shaped leaves of this cyclamen provide interest into the spring.

WINTER ACONITE *ERANTHIS HYEMALIS*

HEIGHT AND SPREAD 4 × 4 in (10 × 10 cm)
SOIL Well-drained; moist but well-drained
HARDINESS Fully hardy
SUN ☼ ☼

The sunny, buttercup-like blooms of this little bulb appear in the depths of winter, often popping up through layers of snow. The flowers are set off by a ruff of leafy bracts and divided green leaves, and the plants will soon spread to form a decorative carpet beneath deciduous trees and shrubs. They prefer a moist soil that does not bake dry in summer but are otherwise easygoing and will perform year after year, needing little help from the gardener.

Set off by green bracts, the winter aconite's yellow flowers sing out from the shade.

DOG'S TOOTH VIOLET *ERYTHRONIUM DENS-CANIS*

HEIGHT AND SPREAD Up to 12 × 8 in (30 × 20 cm)
SOIL Moist but well-drained
HARDINESS Hardy to 5°F (−15°C)
SUN ☼

The nodding pink, white, yellow, or purple spring flowers of this bulb look as if they have been gently swept backward in the breeze, while marbled foliage creates a foil for both the blooms and other shade-lovers such as ferns. Popular cultivars include 'Lilac Wonder', with its lilac-pink blooms, and the golden-flowered E. 'Pagoda'. Alternatively, try the fawn lily, *E. californicum*, which has drooping petals. Plant bulbs in the fall, avoiding areas close to shrubs or trees where the soil will dry out in summer.

Dog's tooth violet flowers have swept-back petals set off by the marbled foliage.

SNOWDROP *GALANTHUS*

HEIGHT AND SPREAD Up to 12 × 4 in (30 × 10 cm)
SOIL Moist but well-drained
HARDINESS Hardy to 5°F (−15°C)
SUN ☼

No shady yard would be complete without this classic winter flower to brighten up a lawn or woodland area during the coldest months. The wealth of species and cultivars offers a wide choice of both plant and flower size, most featuring green patterns on the white petals though a few, such as the Sandersii Group, have yellow markings. While you can plant dry bulbs in the fall, most suppliers offer plants in leaf after flowering, known as "in the green" (see p.75). Plant where the soil will not dry out in summer.

'S. Arnott' has wide-spreading white petals and an inner segment with a green marking.

HYACINTH *HYACINTHUS ORIENTALIS*

HEIGHT AND SPREAD Up to 20 × 6 in (40 × 15 cm)
SOIL Well-drained; moist but well-drained
HARDINESS Hardy to 14°F (−10°C)
SUN ☼ ☼

Loved for their large, colorful flowers and sweet fragrance, hyacinths make a great addition to spring borders and patio pots. There is a huge choice of flower colors, ranging from pink and blue to purple, white, and yellow, with some featuring striped petals in more than one shade. The blooms are surrounded by a skirt of wide, strap-shaped leaves. Plant the bulbs in the fall in soil that will not be too wet over winter, and where you can enjoy the flowers' scent. You may need to stake the heavy blooms.

'Queen of the Pinks' bears bright pink, fragrant flowers decorated with darker stripes.

ENGLISH HYACINTH *HYACINTHOIDES NON-SCRIPTA*

HEIGHT AND SPREAD Up to 12 × 4 in (30 × 10 cm)
SOIL Well-drained
HARDINESS Fully hardy
SUN ☼ ☼

The sight of a woodland filled with English hyacinths in spring is a glory to behold, and they can produce a similar effect on a smaller scale in the yard. Unlike the larger Spanish hyacinths, whose blooms are borne each side of taller stems, the violet-blue, more delicate flowers of this species hang gracefully from one side of the stem. In the UK, these wildflowers are protected by law. Plant under deciduous trees and shrubs in the fall.

Where happy, the English hyacinth will soon spread to form carpets of scented spring flowers.

SUMMER SNOWFLAKE *LEUCOJUM AESTIVUM*

HEIGHT AND SPREAD 16 × 8 in (40 × 20 cm)
SOIL Moist but well-drained
HARDINESS Fully hardy
SUN ☼ ☼

How this elegant bulb acquired its common name is a mystery, since it is often in bloom in late winter and has usually died down by the time summer arrives. Grown for its snowdrop-shaped white blooms with green tips, which hang gracefully from tall stems among the strappy green leaves, it is happy in light shade close to trees and shrubs. Plant in the fall. This plant rarely suffers from pests or diseases, so you can expect healthy growth to reappear each year.

The popular cultivar 'Gravetye Manor' has slightly larger flowers than the species.

MARTAGON LILY *LILIUM MARTAGON*

HEIGHT AND SPREAD Up to 5 × 1 ft (1.5 × 0.3 m)
SOIL Well-drained; moist but well-drained
HARDINESS Fully hardy
SUN ☼ ☼

While some lilies prefer to bask in the sun, the martagon prefers a little shade. The flowers have reflexed petals that were said to look like the turban of the Turkish ruler Sultan Mohammed I, and they hang from slim stems to create a chandelier of blooms in summer. Flower colors include white, yellow, pink, orange, and red, some with speckled petals. Plant these hardy bulbs in late winter or early spring in the ground or in a pot of peat-free potting mix if you have wet soil.

The swept-back petals of the martagon lily reveal pollen-rich anthers that attract bees.

DAFFODIL *NARCISSUS*

HEIGHT AND SPREAD Up to 20 × 6 in (50 × 15 cm)
SOIL Well-drained; moist but well-drained
HARDINESS Fully hardy
SUN ☼ ☼

Daffodils' distinctive blooms with their petal-framed trumpets are synonymous with spring and as there are thousands to choose from, there is a selection ideal for every situation. Plant the taller ones in beds, or use dwarf favorites such as 'Tête-à-tête' and 'Minnow' in pots and window boxes. Combining different types can extend the show from late winter to late spring. All bloom well in the shade of a deciduous tree or shrub, or next to a wall or fence. For the best effect, plant en masse in the fall.

'February Gold', with its bright yellow flowers, is often in bloom from late winter.

SIBERIAN SQUILL *SCILLA SIBERICA*

HEIGHT AND SPREAD 6 × 2 in (15 × 5 cm)
SOIL Well-drained
HARDINESS Fully hardy
SUN ☼ ☼

The Siberian squill is one of the best scillas for shade and will produce its stems of nodding, parasol-shaped bright blue flowers for many weeks in early spring. Perfect for naturalizing in a lawn or beneath the boughs of a deciduous tree, these diminutive plants rapidly form a carpet of colorful blooms. The narrow, strap-shaped green leaves soon fade after flowering. Plant the bulbs in the fall, scattering them in drifts in any area that's in need of spring color, apart from in soils that are wet.

The bright blue flowers of the Siberian squill have darker stripes that add to their charms.

INTRODUCING SHADE-MAKING TREES

Planting new trees will, of course, cast more shade over your yard, but they can have many benefits, such as shielding seating or play areas from hot summer sun, creating a woodland area for quiet reflection, and supporting wildlife. Choosing a tree can be daunting, with such a wide range of sizes, foliage types, and flower colors on offer, but careful planning will help you make the right selection.

A mature apple tree provides a cool seating area, as well as blossoms in spring and delicious fruit in the fall.

A rowan tree offers bright fall berries and a feast for hungry birds to enjoy as temperatures drop.

LOOKING GOOD

When selecting a new tree, consider what you want from it, be that spring flowers, cool leafy shade in summer, fall color, winter berries, or all of these attributes. Alternatively, you may be looking for evergreen structure to mask a neighbor's window and offer year-round privacy.

Many trees provide a range of beautiful features at various times of the year, so make a list of when those you like put on their most spectacular displays. This will help you select multi-seasonal specimens or a few trees that complement one another.

CHECKING THE SIZE

One of the most important checks to make before purchasing a new tree is its size. Most nurseries will give the approximate height and spread of a tree after 10 or 20 years and when fully mature. Trees are a long-term investment, both financially and in the environmental benefits they offer, and it is always best to plant one where it can reach maturity without excessive pruning, allowing you to enjoy it for many years to come. Remember to look at the width as well as the height, since a spreading tree can fill a small yard, even if it is only a few yards tall. Also check how quickly your tree will grow; you may want to buy a larger specimen if it will take a long time to fulfill the functions you are hoping for. However, younger trees tend to establish more quickly than mature ones, so ask a specialized nursery for advice if you are unsure what size would be best for you.

A colorful Japanese maple (*Acer palmatum*) makes a bold focal point in a small yard from spring to fall.

LIGHT AND SOIL

If your yard is already shady, you will need a tree that can cope with low light conditions (see pp.84–87); sun-loving trees such as Japanese cherries (*Prunus* species), laburnums, *Koelreuteria*, and many conifers will reach for the light and become misshapen if you grow them in shade. They may also fail to fruit and flower very well, so check the light levels that your desired plants require before you buy.

Acer griseum will put on its best show of foliage and peeling bark when grown on slightly acidic soil.

Soil preferences are also important to consider. While many trees are not too picky, some require acid soil to thrive (see p.25), and only a few backyard species are adapted to thrive in wet, boggy conditions.

NEED TO KNOW
Trees growing over adjoining yards can cause disputes, so look up the spread of the tree and plant it at least half that distance away from the boundary, also checking that it will not cast shade over neighbors' windows.

BEST POSITIONS

When deciding where to place a tree, think of using it to create a focal point, perhaps within a bed or border, at the end of a path, or in the center of a lawn. In a small yard, you will probably want to see it from the main windows of the house, but make sure it won't throw your whole plot into shade. In the northern hemisphere, placing it on the south side will shade more of your yard than planting it on the north side, where it will block the light only beneath its canopy because the sun will never be behind it; in the southern hemisphere, the opposite applies.

The roots of a tree can undermine the foundations of a house if planted too close to it. Check the mature width of your tree's canopy, which will be roughly equal to the width of the root system; for example, a small tree that is 10 ft (3 m) wide can be safely planted 12–15 ft (4–5 m) from the house.

The soil next to a wall or fence is dry, so plant a tree at least 3 ft (1 m) away from these barriers, where it can thrive.

Plant a good distance away from a wall or fence, as the soil close to it will be dry and roots will struggle to establish.

PLANTING A TREE

Planting a tree well and taking care of it until the roots have established will help ensure that it thrives and grows into a beautiful mature specimen. Before buying, check that your site and soil are appropriate for your chosen tree (*see p.80*), and ensure you water it well during dry spells after planting. The method shown here is for bare-root, root-balled, or container-grown trees, and the best time to plant them is between late fall and early spring.

Planting well ensures your tree will establish quickly and thrive for many years.

CHOOSING A TREE

Specialized tree nurseries usually offer an option of bare-root, root-balled, or container-grown plants. Bare-root trees have been grown in a nursery bed for a few years and are then dug out while dormant from late fall to early spring, and sent to you with their roots wrapped in burlap or similar material. These tend to be the cheapest option.

Semi-mature deciduous trees and conifers are available as root-balled trees. They have also been grown in the ground but their roots are contained in a ball of soil to preserve the fine feeder root system when they are dug out of the ground. These trees are available from fall to early spring but are more expensive than bare-root types because they tend to be older and have a good fibrous root system that will establish more quickly.

Trees that have been raised in the nursery in a container may be more expensive than the other options, but they are available all year and can be planted at any time, except when the ground is frozen or waterlogged.

Container-grown trees can be planted at any time of the year, unless the soil is frozen or waterlogged.

PLANTING METHOD

YOU WILL NEED Tree • Bucket • Spade Fork • Mycorrhizal fungi • Watering can or hose • Stake (for large trees)

1 Place your tree in a bucket of water for about an hour to soak the root ball. Meanwhile, dig a square hole three times as wide as the container or root ball and the same depth. Use a fork to loosen the soil around the sides of the hole. Apply some mycorrhizal fungi to the bottom of the hole to promote good root growth, but do not add any organic matter or compost, which may cause the tree to sink once planted, nor any fertilizer.

2 Remove the container if there is one and place the root ball in the hole. Lay a cane or the spade across the hole to check that the point where the roots meet the stem will be level with, or slightly above, the soil surface once the tree is planted.

3 Gently loosen the roots if they are coiled around the sides of the root ball, then set the tree in the hole. Refill around it with the excavated soil, again checking that it is at the correct level, and firm down the soil to remove any large air pockets. Water well. Apply a 2–3 in (5–8 cm) layer of bark chips over the soil, leaving a 4 in (10 cm) gap around the trunk.

4 Irrigate newly planted trees once or twice a week during dry spells for three years after planting. Using a large watering can fitted with a rose head or a hose on a gentle setting, apply enough water for it to filter down to the roots at lower levels. This method mimics a rain shower and will sustain the tree's roots without dislodging the soil around them.

TOP TIP MAKE SURE AN AREA AT LEAST 3 FT (1 M) IN DIAMETER AROUND YOUR TREE IS FREE OF WEEDS AND OTHER PLANTS WHILE IT IS ESTABLISHING SO THE ROOTS DO NOT HAVE TO COMPETE FOR WATER AND NUTRIENTS.

STAKING A TREE

Many small or young trees will not need staking, and gentle rocking in the wind will encourage the roots to grow and secure the tree in the ground. However, tall trees and those with a dense crown of leaves and small root ball will need

Use a tree tie to secure the stake to the tree trunk, about one-third of the way up.

staking. To do this, hammer in a stake at a 45-degree angle, so it meets the tree one third of the way up the trunk, and is driven at least 2 ft (60 cm) into the ground. Make sure it is leaning into the prevailing wind direction to secure the tree firmly during blustery weather.

Use a tree tie to secure the stake to the tree and check it every year, loosening the tie as necessary. The roots should establish in two to three years, when the stake can be removed.

SMALL TREES FOR SHADE

Trees come in all shapes and sizes, and while some species will grow into towering giants that would be better suited to parkland or an extensive country landscape, others make beautiful features in the smallest of spaces and deliver all the benefits of their larger cousins. Ideal for small to medium-size yards, the selection here will perform well in low light conditions, making them good choices if your plot is already shaded by buildings or mature trees.

FIELD MAPLE *ACER CAMPESTRE*

HEIGHT AND SPREAD Up to 26 × 10 ft (8 × 3 m)
SOIL Moist but well-drained
HARDINESS Fully hardy
SUN ☼ ☼

The field maple makes a medium-size deciduous tree, but as it is well adapted to being clipped you can control its size by regular pruning or coppicing (see p.135). It also makes a food-rich wildlife hedge. The lobed green leaves are flushed with red when they emerge alongside tiny white flowers in spring. In the fall, the foliage lights up the yard when it turns yellow or orange-red; winged fruits appear at the same time. For a tall, slim tree, try 'William Caldwell'. Prune from late fall to midwinter.

This long-lived tree offers privacy well into the fall.

PAPERBARK MAPLE *ACER GRISEUM*

HEIGHT AND SPREAD Up to 26 × 26 ft (8 × 8 m)
SOIL Well-drained; moist but well-drained
HARDINESS Hardy to 5°F (−15°C)
SUN ☼ ☼

This eye-catching, slow-growing tree really comes into its own in the fall and winter, when the elegant, divided green leaves fire up in shades of orange and scarlet before falling to reveal the decorative stems in all their glory. The bark on mature trees is cinnamon-colored and peels off year-round in thin, paperlike layers. There are few trees that can compete with its stunning good looks when silhouetted against a cold, wintry sky. Prune only to remove dead, diseased, or crossing branches in midwinter.

The beautiful, peeling bark of this decorative maple gives rise to its common name.

JAPANESE MAPLE *ACER PALMATUM*

HEIGHT AND SPREAD Up to 26 × 26 ft (8 × 8 m)
SOIL Moist but well-drained; neutral to acid
HARDINESS Fully hardy
SUN ☼

The choice of Japanese maples is vast and most make lovely trees for small yards or large pots. Grown for their finely cut foliage and fiery fall tints, they prefer neutral to acid soil and some shade to prevent the delicate leaves from scorching. Most cultivars are smaller than the species, reaching about 16 ft (5 m) in height, and they are slow-growing, so buy a tree that almost fits its allotted space. The graceful canopies are best left unpruned; just remove dead, diseased, or wayward stems in late winter.

'Ōsakazuki' produces lobed, bright green leaves that turn scarlet in the fall.

SERVICEBERRY *AMELANCHIER*

HEIGHT AND SPREAD Up to 26 × 26 ft (8 × 8 m)
SOIL Well-drained; moist but well-drained
HARDINESS Fully hardy
SUN ☼ ☼

Many *Amelanchier* species and cultivars are good choices for small yards, their bronze young foliage, spring flowers, red or purple summer fruits, and beautiful fall color providing a long period of interest. Among the best are *A.* × *grandiflora* 'Ballerina' with its pure white spring blossom and 'Robin Hill', which bears flowers that open from pink buds and fade to white. Both offer fiery leaves in the fall before they drop. Prune lightly, if necessary, in late winter or early spring, to remove dead, diseased or crossing stems.

'Ballerina' is a small, compact tree with white flowers and bright fall leaf color.

REDBUD *CERCIS CANADENSIS* 'FOREST PANSY'

HEIGHT AND SPREAD Up to 26 × 26 ft (8 × 8 m)
SOIL Moist but well-drained
HARDINESS Hardy to 5°F (−15°C)
SUN ☼ ☼

Grown for its heart-shaped, deep purple leaves, this small deciduous tree makes a beautiful focal point all year round. The foliage is a spectacular sight in the fall, when it turns orange, bronze, and red-purple before falling; in early spring, purple or pink flowers appear on the bare stems. It prefers a warm, sheltered spot but tolerates light shade. For a small space, choose a multi-stemmed tree, which will remain more compact than one grown on a single trunk. Prune, if necessary, in late winter.

Heart-shaped purple foliage that fires up in the fall creates a show-stopping display.

CHINESE DOGWOOD *CORNUS KOUSA* VAR. *CHINENSIS*

HEIGHT AND SPREAD Up to 22 × 16 ft (7 × 5 m)
SOIL Well-drained; moist but well-drained; neutral to acid
HARDINESS Hardy to 5°F (−15°C)
SUN ☼ ☼

Eye-catching in late spring and early summer when the leafy stems are adorned with large white or pink-tinted flowers, this small deciduous tree is the perfect choice for a yard with slightly acidic or neutral soil. The flowers comprise tiny green blooms surrounded by white or pink petal-like bracts; they are followed in the fall by fruits resembling strawberries. The fall show includes fiery red and orange leaves. Prune lightly in late winter or early spring, removing dead, diseased, and crossing stems.

Large white bracts surround tiny green flowers on Chinese dogwoods in early summer.

CORNELIAN CHERRY *CORNUS MAS*

HEIGHT AND SPREAD 13 × 13 ft (4 × 4 m)
SOIL Moist but well-drained
HARDINESS Fully hardy
SUN ☼ ☼

This small deciduous tree will stand quietly in the yard from spring to summer, when it's adorned with small green leaves and oval, red, edible fruits, loved by birds. The foliage then turns red-purple in the fall, but this little tree leaves the best performance until last, creating a breath-taking sight in midwinter when the stems are stripped of foliage and studded with bright yellow flowers. Fully hardy and adapted to most soils, except wet, it can be pruned in early spring after flowering to keep it neat and compact.

Golden-yellow flowers on the bare stems of this *Cornus* set the garden alight in winter.

CORKSCREW HAZEL *CORYLUS AVELLANA* 'CONTORTA'

HEIGHT AND SPREAD 16 × 16 ft (5 × 5 m)
SOIL Well-drained; moist but well-drained
HARDINESS Fully hardy
SUN ☼ ☀

Making an eye-catching feature in winter and early spring, this little tree features twisted stems and long, yellow catkins that dangle from the branches. The slightly contorted, heart-shaped green leaves turn buttery yellow in the fall, when hazelnuts may appear, too. Site it where the winter sun will catch the stems and catkins; this tough plant will not balk if other trees shade it in summer. The cultivar 'Red Majestic' has dark purple leaves and purple-pink catkins. Remove straight stems when you see them.

Golden catkins hang from the twisted stems of this hazel from late winter.

HAWTHORN *CRATAEGUS LAEVIGATA*

HEIGHT AND SPREAD Up to 26 × 26 ft (8 × 8 m)
SOIL Moist but well-drained
HARDINESS Fully hardy
SUN ☼ ☀

Tough and able to cope with exposed sites in windswept yards, this deciduous tree has lobed green leaves that unfurl on spiny stems in spring, followed by white or pink flowers, loved by bees. The red fall berries, which appear just as the foliage turns yellow and red, provide a food source for many types of bird. 'Paul's Scarlet' is one of the most attractive pink forms, but its double flowers are less appealing to pollinators. Prune lightly in late winter or early spring to remove dead, diseased, and crossing stems.

In spring, 'Paul's Scarlet' bears rich pink double flowers that contrast well with the leaves.

COMMON HOLLY *ILEX AQUIFOLIUM*

HEIGHT AND SPREAD 20 × 13 ft (6 × 4 m)
SOIL Moist but well-drained
HARDINESS Fully hardy
SUN ☀ ☀

Providing year-round interest with their glossy evergreen leaves, hollies make a beautiful addition to a yard. Those with spiny-edged foliage can also be used as a security barrier. Male and female flowers appear on separate plants but only the females produce the fall berries, loved by birds. Male plants—necessary for pollination of the female blooms—are abundant in the wild so you don't need to buy one for your yard. Alternatively, opt for a self-fertile cultivar such as 'J. C. van Tol'.

'J. C. van Tol' is self-fertile and has smooth-edged evergreen leaves and red berries in the fall.

MAGNOLIA *MAGNOLIA* SPECIES

HEIGHT AND SPREAD Up to 20 × 20 ft (6 × 6 m)
SOIL Moist but well-drained; neutral to acid
HARDINESS Fully hardy
SUN ☼ ☀

There is a host of *Magnolia* species and cultivars ideal for small yards, most growing to no more than 20 ft (6 m) in height, many even smaller, so simply choose a flower color you like and a size to suit. All prefer acid soil, with shade from early-morning sun and shelter from hard frosts, which can damage the blooms. *M. stellata*, with its starry white flowers, and cultivars of *M.* × *soulangeana*, the flowers of which are usually white or pink, are among the best choices. Prune in midsummer, if needed.

The pale pink blooms of *Magnolia* × *soulangeana* appear before the leaves in spring.

CRAB APPLE *MALUS*

HEIGHT AND SPREAD Up 26 × 20 ft (8 × 6 m)
SOIL Moist but well-drained
HARDINESS Fully hardy
SUN ☼ ☼

Crab apples offer a range of features that decorate the yard for much of the year, and most are well-behaved small trees. Pollinator-friendly, they produce an abundance of white or pink blossoms in spring, followed by red or yellow edible fruits in the fall. Some, such as 'Prairie Fire' and 'Royalty', have dark purple leaves, while others produce green foliage; nearly all offer good fall color. For jelly-making, try the larger-fruited JELLY KING or 'John Downie'. If needed, prune in late winter.

'Evereste' produces white flowers from red buds and masses of fruit in the fall.

PERSIAN IRONWOOD *PARROTIA PERSICA*

HEIGHT AND SPREAD Up to 26 × 26 ft (8 × 8 m)
SOIL Well-drained; moist but well-drained
HARDINESS Fully hardy
SUN ☼ ☼

Often grown as a multi-stemmed specimen, the Persian ironwood makes a sculptural feature, its wavy-edged, oval, green leaves turning bright yellow, orange, and red in the fall. In the depths of a cold winter, it offers another surprise when the unusual red flowers, which lack petals, dangle from the bare twigs like tassels. The gray bark also flakes off to reveal lighter patches beneath, drawing the eye before the leaves hide all the stems bar the trunk in spring. Prune in late winter or early spring.

Grown for its stunning fall colors, the Persian ironwood also bears unusual winter flowers.

YEW *TAXUS BACCATA*

HEIGHT AND SPREAD 26 × 26 ft (8 × 8 m)
SOIL Moist but well-drained
HARDINESS Fully hardy
SUN ☼ ☼ ☼

The species of this versatile evergreen will grow into a large tree in time, but there are beautiful dwarf cultivars and all thrive in low light conditions and most soils. You can also trim yew each year to keep it in check or grow it as a hedge or topiary. Dwarf cultivars include 'Fastigiata Aureomarginata', a columnar tree with gold-edged leaves, 'Standishii', with golden foliage, and the green-leaved 'Fastigiata Robusta'. Prune at any time, except between spring and midsummer when birds are nesting.

'Standishii' is a compact, columnar tree that can be grown in shade, close to other trees.

ROWAN *SORBUS AUCUPARIA*

HEIGHT AND SPREAD Up 26 × 16 ft (8 × 5 m)
SOIL Well-drained; moist but well-drained
HARDINESS Fully hardy
SUN ☼ ☼

Some rowans may outgrow their space in a yard but AUTUMN SPIRE and 'Vilmorinii' are more compact. Like all rowans, they produce finely divided leaves that offer red, yellow, and purple fall color, at the same time that clusters of round berries appear. AUTUMN SPIRE is more columnar than most and produces yellow fruits, while those of 'Vilmorinii' are dark red, fading to pinkish-white. The fruits form after the flat heads of fluffy, white flowers, loved by bees, appear in summer. Prune in late winter.

'Autumn Spire' produces yellow berries and purple, red, and yellow fall leaves.

CLIMBING HIGH

Many climbing plants are adapted to shady sites and use their ability to scale tall plants and structures to reach the sun while their roots enjoy the cool, moist soil conditions below. They take up very little space in the ground and can be squeezed into the smallest of spaces, where you can use them to dress walls, fences, pergolas, arches, and arbors with curtains of lush foliage and flowers. Climbers scale their hosts in a variety of ways, so check their needs before planting and install supports as required.

Use twining, shade-tolerant climbers such as clematis to decorate a trellis panel with foliage and flowers.

CHOOSING AND PLANTING A CLIMBER

Before buying a climber, check first that it will perform well in your soil and the light levels it will receive. Shade-tolerant plants include some beautiful climbing and rambling roses and other favorites such as clematis, jasmine, and honeysuckle, many of which will suit a confined space (*see pp.90–95*). However, read the labels carefully to check plants' final heights and spreads, as some of the larger species, including the chocolate vine (*Akebia*), Virginia creeper (*Parthenocissus*), and the appropriately named mile-a-minute (*Fallopia baldschuanica*), will quickly swamp a small space.

The soil close to a wall, fence, or vertical screen is often very dry, so plant your climber about 18 in (45 cm) away from it where conditions will be more favorable. Lean the root ball slightly toward the support and use canes to guide the stems to it. Once they reach the wires or trellis, you may need to tie them on initially before they begin to twine of their own accord.

Plant about 18 in (45 cm) away from a fence or wall where the soil is dry and guide the stems toward it with canes.

Affix wooden battens to a wall before attaching a trellis panel to them to create a space for the stems to wrap around it.

For twiners, screw vine eyes to the top and bottom of a post, or in a horizontal line along a fence, and stretch sturdy wire between them.

INSTALLING A SUPPORT

It's important to provide an adequate support for twining climbers and roses to allow them to scramble along a fence or wall, or cover an arch, pergola, or arbor. The stems of large climbers can be heavy, so ensure you use sturdy wires, vine eyes, and trellis to prevent them falling down and breaking or causing someone an injury.

Attach heavy-duty wires to vine eyes in horizontal lines at 12 in (30 cm) intervals up a fence or wall. Simply twist the wire around one vine eye and stretch it across to a second one, then insert the wire and twist to secure it. The posts of a pergola or arbor can

be wired up in the same way. Tensioned wire trellis kits, which comprise stainless steel wires attached to durable mounts, are also available and recommended for training large climbers on a wall or fence.

Trellis is another option for twining climbers and climbing roses. Attach the panels to horizontal wooden battens fixed to your wall or fence, which will create a space behind to allow the climber's stems to twine around them.

TOP TIP THE AERIAL ROOTS OF IVY AND OTHER SELF-CLINGING CLIMBERS MAY DAMAGE OLD WALLS WITH POOR OR CRUMBLING MORTAR BUT WILL NOT AFFECT THOSE WITH SOUND MASONRY.

HOW CLIMBERS CLIMB

When selecting a climber, take note of the method by which it climbs, as this will determine the type of support it requires.

TWINING TENDRILS AND STEMS Twining climbers use leaf stalks and tendrils or stems to wrap around their supports, and will need wires, trellis, canes, or a shrub or tree to climb up. This group includes clematis, star jasmine (*Trachelospermum*), and honeysuckle (*Lonicera*).

HOOKS Climbing and rambling roses ascend by hooking their thorny stems onto plants, trees, or trellis. Climbing rose stems need to be tied onto wires or trellis each year to keep them in place, while ramblers will climb unaided up a tree once the stems reach the lower branches.

STEM ROOTS AND ADHESIVE PADS Plants such as ivy, Boston ivy, and Virginia creeper (*Parthenocissus* species) and climbing hydrangeas (*Hydrangea anomala* subsp. *petiolaris*) cling to their supports via stem roots or adhesive pads. These plants are the easiest to grow and require no additional supports to climb up a structure.

CLIMBERS FOR SHADY SPACES

The perfect plants to create a cool, leafy ambience, shade-loving climbers will dress up boundary walls and fences with their flowers and foliage or twine through trees and shrubs to extend their hosts' season of interest. Here is a selection of some of the best climbing plants, which you can combine to create a year-round display. Just remember that many will need a support such as wires or a trellis to help them climb (*see p.89*).

CHOCOLATE VINE *AKEBIA QUINATA*

HEIGHT AND SPREAD 26 × 6½ ft (8 × 2m)
SOIL Moist but well-drained
HARDINESS Fully hardy
SUN ☼ ☼

Given space for its twining stems to reach up and out, the chocolate vine makes a beautiful leafy screen, its purple-brown flowers emitting a spicy fragrance as they bloom in late spring. It is semi-evergreen in mild winters, the bright green foliage taking on purple tints when temperatures fall. In cold winters the leaves drop and reappear in spring. In the fall, purple, sausage-shaped fruits appear. This easygoing plant climbs through shrubs or trees, or along wires. Prune after flowering.

The chocolate vine lives up to its name when the purple-brown flowers appear in spring.

CORAL PLANT *BERBERIDOPSIS CORALLINA*

HEIGHT AND SPREAD 13 × 3 ft (4 × 1 m)
SOIL Well-drained
HARDINESS Hardy to 23°F (−5°C)
SUN ☼ ☼

You may have to search for the coral plant, since it is not widely grown, but in a sheltered yard it makes an eye-catching statement clinging to wires on a wall or fence, or threaded through a tree. The twining woody stems are covered with dark green, slightly spiny, evergreen foliage and in summer and early fall they are dressed with clusters of deep red flowers that lend a tropical look to the yard. It is a good choice for a mild area where temperatures rarely fall below 23°F (−5°C).

The dainty, red flowers of the coral plant look like strings of red beads when in bud.

PURPLE APPLE BERRY *BILLARDIERA LONGIFLORA*

HEIGHT AND SPREAD 6½ × 6½ ft (2 × 2m)
SOIL Well-drained; moist but well-drained; neutral to acid
HARDINESS Hardy to 23°F (−5°C)
SUN ☼ ☼

A twining evergreen perennial, this plant can be grown outside in a sheltered yard that doesn't experience hard frosts. In colder areas, plant it in a pot and overwinter indoors. In midsummer, the lance-shaped, dark green leaves are joined by pale yellow-green bell-shaped flowers, followed in the fall by violet fruits that last for many weeks. The cultivars 'Fructo Alba' and 'Cherry Berry' produce white and red fruits respectively. This climber will thrive in a neutral to acid soil on a partly shaded wall.

Bright violet fruits create an eye-catching feature when they appear in the fall.

CLEMATIS *CLEMATIS*

HEIGHT AND SPREAD Up to 26 × 13 ft (8 × 4 m)
SOIL Moist but well-drained
HARDINESS Hardy to 5°F (−15°C)
SUN ☼ ☀

Most clematis thrive in an area where their roots are in cool shade but their upper flowering stems receive more sunlight. Among the best that tolerate part shade are the large, sprawling C. *montana*, which produces scented white flowers in late spring; the more compact C. *alpina*, which also flowers in spring; C. 'Bill Mackenzie' with its bright yellow late summer flowers followed by fluffy seed heads; and C. 'Nelly Moser', the striped summer flowers of which can fade if grown in too much sun.

'Nelly Moser' has striped pink flowers that retain their rich color when it is grown in shade.

COMMON IVY *HEDERA HELIX*

HEIGHT AND SPREAD Up to 26 × 13 ft (8 × 4 m)
SOIL Well-drained; moist but well-drained
HARDINESS Fully hardy
SUN ☼ ☼ ☀

This vigorous, self-clinging climber is best for wildlife gardens or areas where its stems will not cause damage to brickwork with old pointing. Many ivy cultivars will create an evergreen screen of lobed foliage in deep shade and dry soils, while variegated forms brighten gloomy corners. The nectar-rich, greenish-yellow flower heads are perfect for pollinators and the black berries are a favorite with many birds. Look out for the smaller cultivars such as 'Midas Touch' and 'Teardrop' if space is limited.

'Teardrop' has dainty, unlobed green foliage and is ideal for a small yard or container.

HOPS *HUMULUS LUPULUS*

HEIGHT AND SPREAD 26 × 8 ft (8 × 2.5 m)
SOIL Moist but well-drained
HARDINESS Fully hardy
SUN ☼ ☼

Common hops are generally grown for beer-making, but more decorative cultivars such as 'Aureus', with golden foliage, are ideal for yards. This deciduous perennial has twining stems of lobed leaves and drooping, greenish-yellow, cone-like flowers followed by attractive seed heads. 'Aureus' needs more sun than the species and may lose its bright color in full shade. However, both are easy to grow and will cover an arch or wires on a fence within one growing season. Cut stems to ground level in spring.

Hops will cover a wall, fence, or arch with their lobed foliage and decorative flowers.

CLIMBING HYDRANGEA
HYDRANGEA ANOMALA SUBSP. *PETIOLARIS*

HEIGHT AND SPREAD 26 × 26 ft (8 × 8 m)
SOIL Moist but well-drained
HARDINESS Hardy to 5°F (−15°C)
SUN ☼ ☼ ☀

Easygoing and self-clinging, this deciduous climber is ideal for a shady wall or fence, its spreading stems providing a leafy screen from spring to fall. The oval green foliage offers a foil for the summer flower heads, which consist of small, fertile blooms surrounded by large, white, sterile flowers. Tolerant of most soils and deep shade, it is a great plant for any yard that has space for it. Prune after flowering in late summer or early fall.

White lace cap flower heads decorate the climbing hydrangea throughout the summer.

WINTER JASMINE *JASMINUM NUDIFLORUM*

HEIGHT AND SPREAD 8 × 8 ft (2.5 × 2.5 m)
SOIL Well-drained
HARDINESS Hardy to 5°F (−15°C)
SUN ☼ ◐

While summer-flowering jasmines thrive in full sun, the winter jasmine is tolerant of shadier conditions. The long, arching stems of this vigorous shrub need to be tied onto wires or a trellis to cover a wall or fence. Clothed with small, divided foliage, the plant creates a leafy screen from spring to fall, after which the bare green stems light up with unscented, bright yellow flowers through to early spring. Prune stems to strong buds after flowering; remove about a quarter of the older shoots on mature plants.

Winter jasmine will brighten up a shady wall with a profusion of cheerful golden blooms.

HONEYSUCKLE *LONICERA PERICLYMENUM*

HEIGHT AND SPREAD 20 × 3 ft (6 × 1 m)
SOIL Moist but well-drained
HARDINESS Fully hardy
SUN ☼ ◐

This classic cottage-garden favorite will fill the air with its sweet scent when the fragrant, creamy-white and purple, pink, or yellow tubular flower heads appear in summer. They are followed by small red berries in late summer and fall. The flowers are loved by moths, butterflies, and other pollinators, while birds will feast on the berries. The oval foliage of this deciduous climber is green. Cut back established plants in late summer, removing a third of the older stems.

The cultivar 'Serotina' has fragrant, deep purple-red and yellow flowers.

VIRGINIA CREEPER *PARTHENOCISSUS*

HEIGHT AND SPREAD Up to 40 × 26 ft (12 × 8 m)
SOIL Moist but well-drained
HARDINESS Hardy to 5°F (−15°C)
SUN ☼ ◐

Most *Parthenocissus* species are tolerant of some shade, their sprawling, self-clinging stems soon covering a house wall. The Chinese Virginia creeper, *P. henryana*, is the least vigorous, making its stems of dark green or bronze-tinted divided leaves, decorated with silvery veins, ideal for a boundary fence. *P. quinquefolia* and the Boston ivy, *P. tricuspidata*, offer unrivaled fall color but are suitable only for large yards or house walls, where they will need to be trimmed regularly.

Suitable for large spaces, Virginia creeper produces spectacular fall foliage.

MAGNOLIA VINE *SCHISANDRA GRANDIFLORA*

HEIGHT AND SPREAD Up to 26 × 8 ft (8 × 2.5 m)
SOIL Well-drained
HARDINESS Hardy to 14°F (−10°C)
SUN ☼ ◐

If you are looking for a distinctive climber and enjoy a reasonably mild climate, the magnolia vine will fit the bill. A twining deciduous climber, it is dioecious, which means male and female flowers appear on separate plants—so while the elegant, bell-shaped, white blooms appear on both forms, only females will deliver the beadlike red fall fruits, and they require a male pollination partner close by. Plant next to a sheltered, semi-shaded wall and tie the stems to wires or a trellis while it establishes. Prune in early spring.

The dainty white flowers of the magnolia vine appear on twining stems in summer.

CHINESE HYDRANGEA VINE

SCHIZOPHRAGMA INTEGRIFOLIUM

HEIGHT AND SPREAD 26 × 8 ft (8 × 2.5 m)
SOIL Moist but well-drained
HARDINESS Hardy to 5°F (−15°C)
SUN ☼ ☀

As the common name suggests, this deciduous climber resembles a hydrangea, with small white flowers surrounded by showy petal-like bracts in summer. It also attaches itself to walls and fences via self-clinging aerial roots and the green leaves turn gold in fall. Red- and pink-flowered cultivars are also available. Provide some protection from cold winds in winter and prune after flowering, if necessary.

Large heads of small flowers and teardrop-shaped bracts cover this climber in summer.

STAR JASMINE *TRACHELOSPERMUM JASMINOIDES*

HEIGHT AND SPREAD 26 × 13 ft (8 × 4 m)
SOIL Well-drained
HARDINESS Hardy to 14°F (−10°C)
SUN ☼ ☀

This plant is loved by landscape designers for its twining stems of glossy, dark, evergreen foliage, which turns bronze-red in winter, and clusters of tiny, highly fragrant white summer flowers. Plant it close to seating or a walkway where you can enjoy the scent. It needs no support system, since the stems are self-clinging. The star jasmine is not totally hardy and will perform best in a sheltered spot in a yard where temperatures do not dip too low in winter. Prune after flowering in late summer or early fall.

Ideal for year-round interest, the star jasmine has evergreen leaves and scented flowers.

CRIMSON GLORY VINE *VITIS COIGNETIAE*

HEIGHT AND SPREAD 40 × 13 ft (12 × 4 m)
SOIL Well-drained
HARDINESS Fully hardy
SUN ☼ ☀

If you have the space, use this vigorous deciduous climber to cover a large wall, fence, or pergola with its twining stems of heart-shaped, dark green leaves, brown-felted beneath. While it is fairly unremarkable from spring to summer, in the fall the crimson glory vine's leaves live up to its name, turning bright scarlet and crimson before falling to the ground to create a carpet of color. Tiny greenish summer flowers are followed in fall by bunches of small blue-black inedible berries. Prune it in midwinter.

The large heart-shaped leaves of the crimson glory vine light up the yard in the fall.

JAPANESE WISTERIA *WISTERIA FLORIBUNDA*

HEIGHT AND SPREAD 26 × 5 ft (8 × 1.5 m)
SOIL Moist but well-drained
HARDINESS Fully hardy
SUN ☼ ☀

The pendent clusters of fragrant, pealike flowers create a beautiful sight in early summer when they cover the twining woody stems of this spectacular plant. Wisteria requires sturdy wires or a large pergola to support its heavy limbs as it climbs, and it also needs careful maintenance to promote a flower display. Prune stems in summer to shorten long, whippy growth, and again in midwinter, reducing the stems you cut back in summer to about three buds from a main stem.

Large pendent flower heads create a spectacular effect and their sweet scent fills the air.

ROSES FOR SHADY WALLS

While many roses like basking in the sun, a surprising number of climbers and ramblers will grow happily in some shade. The flowers of a few even prefer low light levels, which prevent the delicate petals from scorching, while rambling roses adapted to growing through trees tolerate shade, too. Check labels and websites before buying to ensure your chosen plants will suit your space, since some grow very large over time. Those listed here represent a small selection of award-winning shade-loving varieties.

ROSA 'BOBBIE JAMES'

HEIGHT AND SPREAD Up to 26 × 13 ft (8 × 4 m)
SOIL Well-drained; moist but well-drained
HARDINESS Fully hardy
SUN ☼ ☼

'Bobbie James' is a large, vigorous rambler that will scale a mature tree, or you can train it along sturdy wires on a boundary wall or fence. The simple green leaves open first, followed in summer by large clusters of small, highly fragrant, semi-double flowers with white petals and bright yellow stamens; they are a magnet for pollinators. Small hips then appear in late summer. Prune to remove dead and diseased growth after flowering in late summer, while taking out one in three of the less productive stems.

Clusters of small white flowers obscure the stems and leaves of this vigorous rambler in summer.

ROSA 'CONSTANCE SPRY'

HEIGHT AND SPREAD Up to 8 × 8 ft (2.5 × 2.5 m)
SOIL Well-drained; moist but well-drained
HARDINESS Fully hardy
SUN ☼ ☼

The large, pink, fully double blooms with a myrrh-like scent cover the tall stems of this rose in summer. It can be grown as a shrub or a climber; when used as the latter, the stems will need to be tied onto sturdy wires or a trellis. Ideal for a small space, this award-winning rose will grow on poor soils as well as in some shade, and the foliage is quite resistant to disease. Prune in late summer when the flowering has finished, removing dead and diseased growth and crossing or weak stems.

Rich pink flowers are an eye-catching feature on this compact climber in summer.

ROSA 'FÉLICITÉ PERPÉTUE'

HEIGHT AND SPREAD Up to 26 × 13 ft (8 × 4 m)
SOIL Well-drained; moist but well-drained
HARDINESS Fully hardy
SUN ☼ ☼

The almost thornless stems of this large rambler are decorated in summer with a beautiful combination of dark pink buds and scented, creamy-white or blush-pink, fully double flowers. These are followed by attractive orange-red hips in the fall. The semi-evergreen, glossy foliage may endure through a mild winter and provides a foil for the small but prolific flowers in summer. Grow this rose up a mature tree or on sturdy wires or a trellis on a fence, wall, or pergola. Prune after flowering.

During summer, the scented, pink-tinged white flowers open from pink buds.

ROSA 'MME ALFRED CARRIÈRE'

HEIGHT AND SPREAD Up to 26 × 8 ft (8 × 2.5 m)
SOIL Well-drained; moist but well-drained
HARDINESS Hardy to 5°F (−15°C)
SUN ☼ ☼

This elegant climber delivers a long season of interest as its white double flowers, sometimes flushed with soft pink tones, appear throughout the summer and early fall. They emit a sweet fragrance, and are followed by red hips. Mme Alfred Carrière is a good choice for a north-facing wall or fence, though the almost thornless stems will need to be tied to sturdy wires or a trellis. To encourage a good show of flowers, deadhead as the blooms fade and prune the stems back hard in winter.

Creamy-colored blooms adorn the stems of this compact climber for many months.

ROSA 'PAUL'S HIMALAYAN MUSK'

HEIGHT AND SPREAD Up to 26 × 13 ft (8 × 4 m)
SOIL Well-drained; moist but well-drained
HARDINESS Fully hardy
SUN ☼ ☼

A good choice for growing through a large, mature tree or along wires on a shady boundary fence or wall, this elegant rose produces clusters of small, fragrant, soft pink flowers in summer among light green leaves. It is a large climber with thorny shoots, so ensure you have space to accommodate it before buying. The blooms are followed by small red hips loved by some birds. Prune in late summer after flowering, removing dead and diseased growth and one in every three old stems on mature plants.

A profusion of small, soft pink flowers draws pollinators to this climber in summer.

ROSA 'SOUVENIR DU DOCTEUR JAMAIN'

HEIGHT AND SPREAD Up to 13 × 8 ft (4 × 2.5 m)
SOIL Well-drained; moist but well-drained
HARDINESS Fully hardy
SUN ☼ ☼

The velvety deep crimson double flowers of 'Souvenir du Docteur Jamain' set it apart from its peers, creating a stunning sight when they open in summer on almost thornless stems. This repeat-flowering scented rose will then bloom into the fall, when orange-red hips appear alongside the blooms and dark green leaves. It is perfect for a shady wall or fence, since too much sun can fade or scorch the flowers. Prune in winter, removing dead, diseased, and crossing stems, as well as some of the older growth.

Sumptuous dark red flowers appear throughout summer and fall on this elegant rose.

ROSA WOLLERTON OLD HALL

HEIGHT AND SPREAD Up to 13 × 13 ft (4 × 4 m)
SOIL Well-drained; moist but well-drained
HARDINESS Fully hardy
SUN ☼ ☼

This large, repeat-flowering climber produces sweetly scented, cup-shaped double flowers throughout summer and fall. They appear on thorny stems among glossy green leaves. Pale apricot in color when they open, the flowers then fade to cream, creating a beautiful two-tone effect, while emitting a citrusy fragrance. Use this rose to cover a shady wall or fence, or grow it over a large pergola, tying the stems to sturdy wires or a trellis. Prune out dead, diseased, and crossing stems in winter.

Apricot blooms open from red-tinted buds and fade to cream, creating a multi-colored effect.

PERFECT POTS

Pots and other containers filled with flowers can lift a shady patio or terrace, adding pops of color where they're most needed and creating another layer of interest. Decorate the house walls and surrounding fences, too, using a selection of climbers (*see pp.90–95*), small pots and hanging baskets filled with shade-tolerant plants. While the options for deep shade are quite limited, there's a huge choice for areas that receive a few hours of direct sun each day, and plants for every season, too.

A potted hydrangea makes an eye-catching display to welcome guests by a front door.

CHOOSING POTS AND CONTAINERS

You can use any container with drainage holes in the base to create a beautiful patio display, but those made from terra-cotta or other porous materials may develop moss, lichens, and liverworts on the surface, especially in damp areas. However, these organisms do plants no harm and can add to the charm of a shady display if you embrace the patinas and textures they create.

Container size is perhaps a more important consideration. Buy those that fit your plants' root balls comfortably, with space below the rim to allow water to collect on the soil surface when you irrigate them. Filling a pot to the brim will mean that water spills over the edge and plants never receive the moisture they need. As large pots hold more potting mix and moisture than smaller ones they need watering less frequently, so they are your best choice if you don't have much time for maintenance.

> **TOP TIP** MANY HOUSEPLANTS ENJOY TIME OUTSIDE IN COOL SHADE. MAKE SURE THEIR POTS HAVE DRAINAGE HOLES AND USE THEM AS A FOIL FOR YOUR SUMMER FLOWERS.

Large terra-cotta pots filled with bright begonias and blue lobelia adorn a partly shady patio.

Include plants such as *Euonymus*, *Gaultheria*, and *Skimmia* that offer color all year round.

MAXIMIZING IMPACT

One large pot filled with a shrub or small tree may be all you need to bring drama to your patio, or you could fill it with an evolving range of seasonal flowers that you change every few months.

Groups of small pots can work well, but few shade plants like dry conditions so they will need frequent watering. For a top designer look, simplify your display with a few large pots, a limited color palette and plants with different leaf and flower shapes and textures to heighten the impact. You can use the smaller shrubs on pp.58–65 or a selection of perennials (see *pp.66–73*), as well as the plants recommended specifically for pots (see *pp.102–109*) to create your plan.

For a year-round display, include some pots planted with leafy evergreens such as *Euonymus*, skimmias, camellias, heucheras, or viburnums, and others that offer seasonal pops of color, which you can add to the group when they are flowering and remove after they fade. If you have space to store the containers in a quiet area, this idea can also save money, allowing you to keep your potted bulbs and perennial plants from year to year. When they are not in flower, place them near an outside tap to remind you to water them.

HIGHER GROUND

Plants in hanging baskets, window boxes, and wall pots may receive more light than those in pots on the ground, which could widen your choices and encourage a more floriferous display. Make sure that wall pots and baskets

Colorful combinations of daffodils, primulas, and violas welcome in spring on a shady windowsill.

are attached securely and that there is no danger of window boxes falling from their sills and causing injury. Shade-tolerant spring bulbs (see *pp.76–79*) and polyanthus primroses can be squeezed into small pots and baskets, while tender trailing fuchsias, begonias, and impatiens will brighten up the summer months. Bugle (*Ajuga*), wintergreen (*Gaultheria procumbens*), and small ivies will see you through the winter.

PLANTING A CRATE FOR SHADE

Simple wooden crates filled with shade-tolerant flowers will transform a gloomy patio or terrace into a feast for the eyes. You can change the flowers each season, refreshing the display every few months, or use small shrubs or perennial plants for a more enduring scheme. Just remember to keep the plants watered, especially during the warmer, drier months. You can buy wooden crates from garden centers and DIY stores and take them to your local recycling center when they're past their best.

HOW TO PLANT A WOODEN CRATE

Choose a single plant species for each crate or combine two or three different types in one large container. This project shows a spring display of double- and single-flowered primroses, which thrive in part shade. Place the crates on gravel or bricks to allow water to drain freely from the base. This will prevent the potting mix from becoming waterlogged and damaging the plants, while helping protect the wood from rotting.

YOU WILL NEED Wooden crate • An old sweatshirt or landscaping fabric • Peat-free potting mix • Scissors • Shade-tolerant plants • Watering can

1 Line a crate with an old sweatshirt that is large enough to cover the base and sides. Alternatively, use a couple of layers of landscaping fabric, available from garden centers.
2 Add potting mix to the crate. Use peat-free multipurpose potting mix for annuals or plants that will be on display for just one or two seasons, or a soil-based potting mix for perennials and shrubs. Fill the crate to about 2 in (5 cm) from the top.
3 Pat down the potting mix and then trim the sweatshirt or landscaping material to fit the crate neatly. Water your plants well about ten minutes before planting them in the container, ensuring that you set them at the same level as they were in their original pots, and that their stems and leaves are not buried under potting mix.
4 Water the plants well, and place in a partly shaded area. Keep the potting mix moist, but not wet, and remove spent flowers regularly to prolong the colorful display.

Double-flowered primulas look like tiny spring-flowering roses packed into this rustic wooden crate.

PLANTING IN POTS

Before you start, check that your pots have drainage holes in the base. Use the same technique for planting as described for crates (you won't need a liner), and remember to leave a space between the potting mix and the rim of the pot to allow water to collect when you irrigate them.

Pots with drainage holes in the base will protect plants from waterlogging.

PLANTING A HANGING BASKET

Plant a beautiful basket to decorate a shady wall or suspend one filled with colorful shade-tolerant blooms from the boughs of a tree. Choose a confection of flowers and foliage from the options on pp.102–109, and in winter, supplement them with small young evergreen shrubs such as *Choisya* and *Skimmia* that will offer temporary color and structure while they are dormant. You can then transplant them into a larger container or border in late spring when they start growing again.

Create this beautiful basket in just a couple of hours and enjoy the display from fall to winter.

An open-sided basket can be used to create a ball of nasturtium and begonia blooms in a shady site.

CHOOSING A BASKET

The easiest baskets to maintain, particularly in the summer months, are those with closed sides, which will retain water longer than open-sided wire- or metal-framed containers. However, if you are happy to water more frequently, the latter allow you to make a ball of foliage and flowers by inserting plants through the gaps in the sides. Baskets are available in a range of

materials, from woven rattan and ceramic to aluminum and stainless steel. Some have integrated liners; you will have to line others with a preformed liner, traditional sphagnum moss (checking it is from a renewable source), or even an old sweatshirt (see p.99).

Whichever style you choose, make sure your basket has drainage holes in it. Their relatively small size and lack of insulation also means the plants housed in them will demand regular watering.

A hose with a long wand attachment allows you to water easily baskets that are difficult to reach.

PLANTING A BASKET

This beautiful winter-flowering arrangement is made using an open-sided basket planted with a young *Skimmia japonica* 'Rubella', cyclamen, violas, small ivies, and heathers (*Erica*). The latter will tolerate light shade but may need more sun when in full growth from spring to late summer. Use the same technique to make a summer basket, supplementing these plants with tender annuals and shrubs such as fuchsias. You will not need a liner for a ceramic basket and can skip steps 1 to 3.

YOU WILL NEED Open-sided hanging basket and liner • Low, wide pot • Piece of recycled plastic • Scissors • Watering can • Newspaper • Small plastic pot (optional)

1 Place the basket in a low, wide terra-cotta pot to stabilize it. If your basket does not have an integrated liner, add one and trim to fit. Cut a few drainage holes in it about ½ in (1 cm) up from the base, which will make a shallow reservoir where water can collect. For permeable liners, lay a sheet of recycled plastic over the base to make a reservoir.

2 Water the plants thoroughly. Fill about a third of the basket with peat-free potting mix and cut crosses in the liner at regular intervals around the sides just above it.

3 Wrap newspaper around the leafy stems of the ivy plants and thread each one from the inside through the crosses, so the root balls are lying on the potting mix surface. Top up the basket with more potting mix, until it is about 2 in (5 cm) from the rim.

4 Plant the skimmia in the center and fill around it with the other plants, packing them in to create a full display—these plants won't grow much in winter so need little room to spread at this time of year. You can also include a small, empty plant pot

TOP TIP USE LARGE BASKETS FOR SHADY SUMMER DISPLAYS—THEY HOLD MORE POTTING MIX AND WATER THAN SMALL ONES SO NEED WATERING LESS OFTEN.

with drainage holes in the base through which to water the basket. Water is prone to spill out of the sides of open baskets and this will ensure it reaches the lower levels of potting mix, wetting it more thoroughly.

5 Baskets need less watering during the winter months when plants are growing slowly or not at all. Summer baskets will need watering every day or two, and a high potash fertilizer applied every two weeks from midsummer.

PLANTS FOR POTS

Many shade-loving plants thrive in pots and will create a colorful display all year round if you combine evergreens for foliage interest with a collection of seasonal flowers. You can supplement the plants recommended here with spring- and summer-flowering bulbs (*see pp.76–79*) and small ferns (*see pp.112–115*), many of which are suitable for growing in containers. Feed perennials and shrubs in pots with a slow-release fertilizer in spring, and start applying a fortnightly liquid feed to annuals and bedding plants a few weeks after planting them (*see also pp.98–101*).

BUGLE *AJUGA REPTANS*

HEIGHT AND SPREAD 6 × 12 in (15 × 30 cm)
SOIL Moist; moist but well-drained
HARDINESS Fully hardy
SUN ☀

Cultivated for both its foliage and its blooms, this plant makes a decorative leafy edge for a large container and delivers added color in spring, when its small blue flowers appear. The evergreen oval leaves may be green, bronze-tinted, purple, or variegated, depending on the cultivar. Easy to grow, bugle needs only moisture and part shade to look its best—in deep shade, colorful forms may revert to green. Its spreading runners make it good for ground cover where the soil does not dry out.

'Burgundy Glow' is popular for its cream-edged, burgundy-tinted foliage and blue flowers.

BEGONIA *BEGONIA*

HEIGHT AND SPREAD Up to 12 × 12 in (30 × 30 cm)
SOIL Moist but well-drained
HARDINESS Tender; hardy to 36°F (2°C)
SUN ☀ ☀

Loved for their colorful, long-lasting flowers and decorative leaves, begonias are the mainstay of summer container displays for shady spaces. With hundreds of types on offer, you can choose from trailing or upright plants and large, showy flowers or small, dainty blooms, some scented, in a vast array of colors. Most begonias are tender, tuberous perennials that will need winter protection indoors if you want to keep them from year to year. Flowering may be reduced in deep shade.

The Million Kisses Series produce pendent flowers and dragon-wing-shaped foliage.

PERENNIAL DAISY *BELLIS PERENNIS*

HEIGHT AND SPREAD 4 × 4 in (10 × 10 cm)
SOIL Well-drained; moist but well-drained
HARDINESS Fully hardy
SUN ☀ ☀

This diminutive plant is used to decorate containers in spring and early summer, when its white, pink, or red flowers bloom for weeks. The cultivated forms produce either traditional daisy flowers or pompom flowers over spoon-shaped green leaves. Tolerant of some drought as well as part shade, these daisies can be combined with spring bulbs and other early-flowering bedding plants to create a dazzling display. You can also plant them in the garden to overwinter and bloom again the next year.

The pink, red, and white pompom flowers of these daisies last for many weeks.

BUTTERFLY BUSH *BUDDLEIA* (DWARF CULTIVARS)

HEIGHT AND SPREAD Up to 5 × 5 ft (1.5 × 1.5 m)
SOIL Moist but well-drained
HARDINESS Fully hardy
SUN ☼ ☀

While some butterfly bushes can reach 10 ft (3 m), a range of smaller hybrids designed for growing in pots is now available. These compact deciduous shrubs produce cone-shaped, scented flowers in shades of white, pink, and purple that attract butterflies and other pollinators. The slim gray-green foliage provides a foil for the long-lasting blooms. These plants tolerate some drought as well as light shade and are very easy to grow, but may perform better long-term if moved to a garden bed after a few years.

'Nanho Purple' is a dwarf butterfly bush that will grow to about 3 ft (1 m) high in a pot.

WINTER CREEPER *EUONYMUS FORTUNEI*

HEIGHT AND SPREAD Up to 3 × 5 ft (1 × 1.5 m)
SOIL Well-drained; moist but well-drained
HARDINESS Hardy to 5°F (−15°C)
SUN ☼ ☀

Winter creeper is a compact evergreen shrub grown for its variegated foliage. The small oval green leaves are edged in gold or cream and often take on pink or red tints as temperatures fall in winter. This plant will grow in quite deep shade, and can be used as a backdrop to more colorful flowers in a container display. While reasonably drought-tolerant, in a pot it performs best when watered regularly from late spring to fall. Clip the stems annually to keep it to the size required.

The leafy winter creeper makes a colorful year-round contribution to a pot display.

FUCHSIA *FUCHSIA*

HEIGHT AND SPREAD Up to 3 × 3 ft (1 × 1 m)
SOIL Moist but well-drained
HARDINESS Tender or hardy to 14°F (−10°C)
SUN ☼ ☀

Fuchsias are ideal for shaded patio pots, putting on a show of dainty flowers for many months in summer and early fall. The pendent blooms come in a wide choice of colors, from white and pink to red and purple. While some of these deciduous or semi-evergreen shrubs are hardy and can be left outside in a sheltered spot all year, others are tender and require overwintering indoors, so check labels before buying. In spring, cut the stems back to encourage new growth and a good flower display.

'Mrs. Popple' is a hardy fuchsia with elegant red and violet-purple summer flowers.

WINTERGREEN *GAULTHERIA PROCUMBENS*

HEIGHT AND SPREAD 6 × 12 in (15 × 30 cm)
SOIL Moist but well-drained; acid
HARDINESS Hardy to 5°F (−15°C)
SUN ☼ ☀

Perfect for a cold-season container display, this pretty evergreen shrub produces rounded leathery leaves that take on red tints in winter, when the small scarlet berries also appear. The fruits are preceded in summer by bell-shaped white or pinkish flowers. Combine this plant with early spring bulbs, other dwarf evergreens, and winter bedding such as violas, planting it in peat-free acidic potting mix. If it outgrows its pot, you can plant it in the yard as ground cover if your soil matches its needs.

Wintergreen produces an abundance of bright red berries amid evergreen foliage.

CHERRY PIE *HELIOTROPIUM ARBORESCENS*

HEIGHT AND SPREAD 12 × 12 in (30 × 30 cm)
SOIL Moist but well-drained
HARDINESS Tender; hardy to 41°F (5°C)
SUN ☀ ☀

Named after its sweetly scented, violet-blue flowers that are said to smell like freshly baked cherry pie, this tender shrub makes an elegant statement in a pot. Offset by crinkly, dark green foliage, the blooms appear for many weeks in summer and introduce color and scent to a container display. While tolerant of some shade, cherry pie may stop flowering in darker sites, so ensure it receives a few hours of sunlight each day. It may also overwinter indoors if kept in a bright but cool position.

Cherry pie produces domed clusters of small, sweetly scented purple flowers in summer.

CORAL BELLS *HEUCHERA*

HEIGHT AND SPREAD Up to 12 × 8 in (30 × 20 cm)
SOIL Moist but well-drained
HARDINESS Fully hardy
SUN ☀

This hardy evergreen perennial will decorate pots all year with its scallop-edged, round foliage. Whatever your color scheme, there's a *Heuchera* to match it, with leaves ranging from purple, silvery-green, and pewter-gray to lime-green and pale orange. Many are bicolored or have marbled patterns, too. In summer, wiry stems of tiny, bell-shaped, pink or white flowers appear above the foliage. All thrive in part shade but may lose their strong colors in darker spots. Keep well watered for best results.

'Obsidian' is loved for the maroon foliage that creates a foil for sprays of white flowers.

FOAMY BELLS × *HEUCHERELLA*

HEIGHT AND SPREAD Up to 12 × 8 in (30 × 20 cm)
SOIL Moist but well-drained
HARDINESS Fully hardy
SUN ☀ ☀

This hybrid between *Heuchera* and *Tiarella* is an evergreen perennial with lobed leaves and slim, wiry stems of small, bell-shaped, pink or white flowers, which appear from late spring to midsummer. A good choice for pots in part shade, it has foliage in different shades of green, often with purple markings, and takes on pinky-bronze tones in winter. Use it as a decorative frill around the edge of a large pot or as a standalone feature, and water it well in summer to keep the foliage looking fresh.

'Tapestry' bears striking green foliage with purple markings below sprays of tiny pink blooms.

PLANTAIN LILY *HOSTA*

HEIGHT AND SPREAD Up to 3 × 3 ft (1 × 1 m)
SOIL Moist but well-drained
HARDINESS Fully hardy
SUN ☀ ☀

Tolerant of quite deep shade, these leafy perennials come in many sizes, from diminutive plants for small containers to large plants that will fill a big pot. Hostas have oval or spear-shaped foliage in colors ranging from dark bottle green to blue-gray and gold, or you can choose one of the many variegated types. Tall stems of lilac or white flowers appear in summer. While hostas can also be grown in beds and borders, planting them in pots can help protect them from slug and snail damage, to which they are prone.

Growing hostas in pots can help protect them from the ravages of slugs and snails.

MOPHEAD HYDRANGEA *HYDRANGEA MACROPHYLLA*

HEIGHT AND SPREAD 4 × 4 ft (1.2 × 1.2 m)
SOIL Moist but well-drained
HARDINESS Fully hardy
SUN ☼ ☼

The colorful flower heads of this deciduous shrub make an eye-catching feature in a summer container display. Some hydrangeas can grow very large but restricting them in a pot will limit their size, while dwarf varieties are also available. Flower colors range from red and pink to white, purple, and blue, but the latter must be planted in acidic potting mix to retain its hue. Give your plants plenty of water and prune the stems lightly to the first or second set of healthy buds each spring.

Blue mophead hydrangeas require both potting mix and fertilizer for acid-loving plants.

BUSY LIZZIE *IMPATIENS*

HEIGHT AND SPREAD Up to 12 × 12 in (30 × 30 cm)
SOIL Moist but well-drained
HARDINESS Tender; hardy to 41°F (5°C)
SUN ☼

Many summer bedding plants like to bask in full sun, but busy lizzies will put on a spectacular show of colorful, round blooms in part shade; they may even flower in deeper shade, but not quite as reliably. The red, pink, mauve, white, or bicolored blooms of this tender annual appear in summer and plants will flower up to the first frosts in the fall if deadheaded regularly. The New Guinea Group of hybrids are larger than the common types and have similar flowers but darker, spear-shaped leaves.

New Guinea busy lizzies grow to about 12 in (30 cm) in height and are mildew-resistant.

SPOTTED DEAD NETTLE *LAMIUM MACULATUM*

HEIGHT AND SPREAD Up to 8 × 18 in (20 × 45 cm)
SOIL Well-drained; moist but well-drained
HARDINESS Fully hardy
SUN ☼ ☼

This spreading perennial is a good choice for cold-season arrangements, where its heart-shaped evergreen leaves will provide a frothy edging to pots and containers—just keep it in a sheltered area to prevent leaf drop. Popular cultivars include 'White Nancy' and 'Beacon Silver', which are grown for their shimmering silver and green foliage. In summer, short spikes of small, hooded, white or pink flowers appear. This leafy plant is also a good choice for ground cover beneath trees, where it will tolerate shade and dry soils.

Dead nettle will soften the edges of a pot all year round with its variegated foliage.

LOBELIA *LOBELIA ERINUS*

HEIGHT AND SPREAD 6 × 8 in (15 × 20 cm)
SOIL Moist but well-drained
HARDINESS Tender; hardy to 34°F (1°C)
SUN ☼ ☼

A popular plant for hanging baskets and window boxes, bedding lobelia comes in trailing and upright forms, both of which produce masses of tiny blooms. Choose from white, pink, purple, or blue flowers, or a bicolored variety. This tender plant will flower continuously from late spring to the first frosts, if kept well watered and deadheaded. It is best grown in part shade, where the cooler conditions help keep the potting mix moist and the plant healthy; in dry soils, it soon turns brown and dies.

Cascading stems of tiny flowers make a colorful frill around pots and hanging baskets.

FORGET-ME-NOT *MYOSOTIS SYLVATICA*

HEIGHT AND SPREAD Up to 12 × 12 in (30 × 30 cm)
SOIL Moist but well-drained
HARDINESS Fully hardy
SUN ☀

This classic spring flower is a must for containers and pots, lending a mass of tiny, bright blue flowers to seasonal displays of spring bulbs and early-flowering perennials. It is a biennial, which means it produces its leaves in the first year and then flowers, sets seed, and dies in the second. The common name is a reference to its tendency to self-seed—you can dig up and pot on any seedlings you find scattered around, ready to use in your container displays the following spring.

The classic blue flowers of forget-me-nots make perfect partners for late spring bulbs.

FIVE SPOT *NEMOPHILA MACULATA*

HEIGHT AND SPREAD 10 × 12 in (25 × 30 cm)
SOIL Moist but well-drained
HARDINESS Hardy to 14°F (−10°C)
SUN ☀ ☀

An eye-catching floriferous annual, in summer this compact plant produces a long-lasting display of bowl-shaped white blooms with five blue-purple spots around the edges. The flowers are set off by green wavy-edged leaves. It will tolerate part shade and is reasonably hardy, often self-seeding around the yard. Very easy to grow, just sow the seeds indoors in spring, plant out after the frosts, and keep plants well-watered. Deadheading will help keep the show going until the fall.

Five spot is named after the blue-purple dots that decorate each of the white flower petals.

TOBACCO PLANT *NICOTIANA*

HEIGHT AND SPREAD Up to 3 × 2 ft (1 × 0.6 m)
SOIL Well-drained; moist but well-drained
HARDINESS Half hardy; hardy to 23°F (−5°C)
SUN ☀ ☀

Perfect for pots close to a seating area, *Nicotiana alata* is a short-lived tender plant that produces large numbers of colorful, trumpet-shaped blooms that emit a delicious scent in the evenings. Spoon-shaped dark green leaves provide a foil for the flowers, which range from pink and red to white and green. The larger woodland tobacco plant (*N. sylvestris*), with heads of long white flowers, also tolerates shade and is suitable for containers that can accommodate its wide-spreading leaves.

N. alata comes in a wide array of flower colors and emits a sweet scent in the evenings.

HOLLY OLIVE *OSMANTHUS HETEROPHYLLUS*

HEIGHT AND SPREAD Up to 3 × 3 ft (1 × 1 m) in a pot
SOIL Well-drained; moist but well-drained
HARDINESS Hardy to 5°F (−15°C)
SUN ☀ ☀

This compact evergreen shrub with spiny-edged dark green foliage makes a handsome specimen for a large pot. Many cultivars have variegated white- or yellow-edged leaves; all produce scented white flowers from late summer to fall, followed by oval, blue-black fruits. The holly olive tolerates quite deep shade, although flowering may be reduced, and creates a textured backdrop for seasonal flower displays. It will take a long time to reach its ultimate height.

This holly lookalike has spiny leaves that deliver year-round color and texture.

ANNUAL PHLOX *PHLOX DRUMMONDII*

HEIGHT AND SPREAD 20 × 20 in (50 × 50 cm)
SOIL Well-drained
HARDINESS Hardy to 23°F (−5°C)
SUN ☼ ☼

Flowering all summer on upright stems, this hardy annual makes a colorful addition to containers. Clusters of small blooms in shades of white, cream, pink, red, and purple appear in summer over green lance-shaped leaves, and persist until mid-fall. Sow seed indoors in spring and plant out the seedlings after the frosts. Keep well-watered and pinch off the top of the stems in early summer to promote more flowering stems. While tolerant of some shade, it will not flower in darker sites.

Heads of small flowers decorate pots all summer if faded blooms are removed regularly.

MOSS PHLOX *PHLOX SUBULATA*

HEIGHT AND SPREAD 6 × 6 in (15 × 15 cm)
SOIL Well-drained; moist but well-drained
HARDINESS Fully hardy
SUN ☼ ☼

A low-growing evergreen perennial, moss phlox is a great choice for small pots on a partly shaded patio. The starry little blooms appear in spring and summer over needlelike green foliage, and flower colors include white, pink, blue, and purple. Clip back the stems after the flowers have faded to keep growth compact and promote new leafy stems to decorate your pots for the rest of the year. Grow this plant in gritty, peat-free potting mix, and also use it as ground cover in cool, shady sites.

An evergreen perennial, moss phlox produces starry flowers in spring and summer.

FORREST'S TAIWAN PIERIS

PIERIS FORMOSA VAR. *FORRESTII*

HEIGHT AND SPREAD Up to 4 × 4 ft (1.2 × 1.2 m) in a pot
SOIL Well-drained; moist but well-drained; acid
HARDINESS Hardy to 5°F (−15°C)
SUN ☼ ☼

For a leafy shrub that offers year-round color, this evergreen pieris is a good choice. It produces glossy, dark green leaves, bright red when young, while sprays of pendent, urn-shaped, cream flowers with a faint scent appear at the same time. After the blooms fade, use the foliage as a backdrop for bright summer flowers. Plant in acidic potting mix and feed each spring with a slow-release fertilizer for acid-loving shrubs.

This pretty pieris produces flowers in spring, just as the red new foliage is emerging.

SWEDISH IVY *PLECTRANTHUS COLEOIDES*

HEIGHT AND SPREAD 6 × 18 in (15 × 45 cm)
SOIL Moist but well-drained
HARDINESS Hardy to 28°F (−2°C)
SUN ☼ ☼

This tender annual's trailing stems create fountains of variegated foliage that will flow over the edges of tall pots, hanging baskets, and window boxes. The green triangular leaves are edged in white and have a citrusy scent when touched. Stems can trail 2 ft (60 cm) or more, but you can clip them back to keep them in check. Swedish ivy tolerates both light shade and short periods of drought, making it ideal for a container. It looks particularly beautiful when paired with brightly colored summer flowers.

Swedish ivy produces trailing stems of variegated foliage that act as a foil for summer flowers.

POLYANTHUS *PRIMULA* POLYANTHUS GROUP

HEIGHT AND SPREAD 10 × 10 in (25 × 25 cm)
SOIL Moist but well-drained
HARDINESS Hardy to 5°F (−15°C)
SUN ☼ ☀

The polyanthus group of primulas are widely available from fall to spring, their red, yellow, white, pink, and purple flowers used as bedding to dress up cold-season containers. The round blooms appear sporadically during the winter, unless the plants are in a sheltered spot such as on a windowsill, but in early spring, they flower more prolifically for many weeks above the textured dark evergreen leaves. Remove dead foliage before it rots to avoid spreading disease to the rest of the plant.

Polyanthus produce their bright, often bicolored blooms from fall to late spring.

SAXIFRAGE *SAXIFRAGA*

HEIGHT AND SPREAD Up to 16 × 8 in (40 × 20 cm)
SOIL Moist but well-drained
HARDINESS Hardy to 5°F (−15°C)
SUN ☼ ☀

Saxifrages comprise a large group of plants but only the small alpines and taller woodland types are sold for garden use. Both tolerate shade and the latter will even grow in deep shade. The woodlanders include the elegant *S. fortunei* and its cultivars, which have scalloped leaves and produce spikes of frothy flowers in late summer and fall. The lower-growing evergreen alpines are ideal for small pots and offer an abundance of small red, pink, or white flowers in spring and summer.

Mossy saxifrages are shade-loving alpines, loved for their spring or summer flowers.

BUTTERFLY ORCHID *SCHIZANTHUS PINNATUS*

HEIGHT AND SPREAD Up to 16 × 16 in (40 × 40 cm)
SOIL Moist but well-drained
HARDINESS Tender
SUN ☼ ☀

While it is not tolerant of deep shade, a spot in dappled light will be sufficient for this tender annual to put on its show of colorful summer flowers. Also known as the poor man's orchid, it has showy blooms in shades of white, pink, and mauve, many bicolored, appearing all summer over ferny green leaves. Sow seeds indoors in spring and plant out after the frosts. To maximize the plant's flowering potential, pinch out the stem tips when seedlings reach about 8 in (20 cm) in height.

Ferny foliage provides a cool contrast to the butterfly orchid's patterned summer flowers.

JAPANESE SKIMMIA

SKIMMIA JAPONICA SUBSP. *REEVESIANA*

HEIGHT AND SPREAD Up to 3 × 3 ft (1 × 1 m)
SOIL Moist but well-drained; acid
HARDINESS Hardy to 5°F (−15°C)
SUN ☼ ☀

This plant is a hermaphrodite, which means that unlike others in the species, it does not need a male plant nearby to pollinate the flowers and produce its profusion of bright red berries. While playing a starring role in a winter container, it offers ornamental value at other times, too, with fragrant white flowers, sometimes tinged red or pink, appearing in mid-spring and the dark green leaves creating a foil for other summer blooms.

Dark evergreen leaves set off the bright red winter berries of this Japanese skimmia.

FOAM FLOWER *TIARELLA CORDIFOLIA*

HEIGHT AND SPREAD 12 × 12 in (30 × 30 cm)
SOIL Moist but well-drained
HARDINESS Hardy to 5°F (−15°C)
SUN ☼ ☀

Named after its cones of tiny white or pink flowers, the foam flower is a compact perennial, ideal for pots in deep shade. The late spring to summer blooms are matched with deeply lobed green foliage, often with dark red markings, which takes on bronze tints in the fall. The leaves may overwinter in sheltered spots. It is easy to care for—just keep the potting mix well watered during the summer. Popular cultivars include 'Spring Symphony', which produces pinkish-white flowers.

'Spring Symphony' features patterned foliage and cones of pink-budded white flowers.

NASTURTIUM *TROPAEOLUM MAJUS*

HEIGHT AND SPREAD Up to 3 × 3 ft (1 × 1 m)
SOIL Well-drained
HARDINESS Hardy to 23°F (−5°C)
SUN ☼ ☀

One of the easiest annuals to grow from seed, nasturtium has long stems of round, wavy-edged leaves and bright summer flowers that will trail from a hanging basket or window box, or climb a plant support in a large pot. Choose from cultivars with plain green or variegated leaves and flowers in colors ranging from yellow to orange and red. While nasturtiums will flower more profusely in full sun, they tolerate part shade. Both the flowers and leaves are edible and have a spicy, peppery taste.

Variegated leaves will brighten a shady space, where flowering may be less abundant.

KOREANSPICE VIBURNUM *VIBURNUM CARLESII*

HEIGHT AND SPREAD Up to 4 × 4 ft (1.2 × 1.2 m) in a pot
SOIL Moist but well-drained
HARDINESS Fully hardy
SUN ☼ ☼ ☀

One of the best viburnums for a container display, this elegant deciduous shrub tolerates full shade and will decorate your garden from spring to fall. The leaves are tinted bronze as they unfurl in early spring, before turning green in summer and finally taking on shades of red in the fall. The pink-budded white flowers with a spicy fragrance appear in spring, followed by red fruits that turn black as they age. Grow in a peat-free, soil-based potting mix in a spot where you can enjoy the scented blooms.

The bee-friendly white blooms of this viburnum open from pink buds.

VIOLA/PANSY *VIOLA*

HEIGHT AND SPREAD 6 × 6 in (15 × 15 cm)
SOIL Moist but well-drained
HARDINESS Fully hardy
SUN ☼ ☀

Bedding pansies and the smaller-flowered violas are usually grown as annuals for winter and spring container displays. The round flowers with yellow eyes and dark markings bring cheer during the cold months, and come in a vast array of colors, from cool whites, purples, and blues to bright oranges, pinks, and reds. The slightly fragrant flowers appear over small evergreen leaves from fall to late spring, but all tend to bloom more profusely as the days grow longer and weather warms.

The pansy's cheerful blooms are guaranteed to brighten up cold-season containers.

MAKE A MODERN FERNERY

Grouping ferns in a fernery to show off their colors and textures is a great way to dress up a cool, dark space in the yard, where many of these beauties will thrive. Initiated by the Victorians, ferneries spurred a craze for collecting these sculptural plants, known at the time as "pteridomania," *pterido* being the Latin word for fern. While most gardeners today are not quite so fanatical, these elegant shade-lovers continue to enthrall us. Making a fernery couldn't be easier—just follow these simple tips.

PREPARING THE WAY

Choose a partly shaded area of the yard by a tree or a structure such as a wall or fence, which will offer the light conditions most ferns enjoy. Some plants will tolerate full shade, so if you want to install your feature in a darker area, check the directory on pp.112–115 for those that will cope. Also assess the soil and select plants that suit your site's conditions.

Check the heights and spreads of your chosen ferns when mature and dig out a bed that will accommodate them comfortably. For the best effect, include three or more of each type, if you have space, which will help create a cohesive design. Then simply plant your ferns at the same depth they were growing at in their original pots.

You can combine small species in a terra-cotta pot to make a tiny fernery for a shady patio or balcony.

The male fern (*Dryopteris filix-mas*) and hard shield fern (*Polystichum aculeatum*) will thrive in areas of dry shade.

FINAL TOUCHES

Use the spaces between your ferns for spring bulbs and shade-loving flowers such as primroses and pulmonarias to add spots of seasonal color. Bulbs can also be planted quite close to deciduous ferns as most bloom before the new fronds unfurl. Once all the planting is complete, add a layer of leaf mold or garden compost over the soil, which will help conserve moisture and suppress weed growth. You could then add a few logs from pruned trees to create a naturalistic woodland-floor effect, and to provide homes for invertebrates and other wildlife.

In a tiny space, you can create a fernery in a large pot. Choose compact species that will not outgrow it, such as small polypodies (*Polypodium vulgare*), the hart's tongue fern (*Asplenium scolopendrium*), and Japanese painted ferns (*Athyrium niponicum*).

Combine ferns that suit your soil and add spots of color with seasonal flowers such as candelabra primulas.

HARDY FERNS

Offering a medley of colors, textures, shapes, and sizes, ferns are a diverse group of plants that thrive in shade. Some will even grow well in the dry, inhospitable conditions beneath mature trees. Guaranteed to add a lush, leafy ambience to your yard, they look beautiful when grouped in a fernery or combined with flowering shade-lovers for a more colorful effect. These ancient nonflowering plants produce microscopic spores instead of seeds, the casings of which can be seen on the undersides of the fronds. Ferns are generally well-behaved and rarely encroach on other plants, but some can grow quite large, so check sizes before buying.

ALEUTIAN MAIDENHAIR *ADIANTUM ALEUTICUM*

HEIGHT AND SPREAD 18 × 18 in (45 × 45 cm)
SOIL Moist but well-drained
HARDINESS Fully hardy
SUN ☀ ☀

This small fern is ideal for filling gaps at the front of a shady border or it can be used to decorate a drystone wall. Deciduous or semi-evergreen during mild winters, the black-stalked, finely divided green fronds appear in sprays that resemble an outstretched hand, while the foliage of the popular cultivar 'Japonicum' is copper-pink when it unfurls in spring, gradually aging to a golden-green as it matures.

This fern copes well with deep shade and the drier soil under deciduous trees.

HART'S TONGUE FERN *ASPLENIUM SCOLOPENDRIUM*

HEIGHT AND SPREAD Up to 24 × 24 in (60 × 60 cm)
SOIL Moist but well-drained
HARDINESS Fully hardy
SUN ☀

The arching strap-shaped fronds of this evergreen fern are said to look like a deer's tongue. In the species, they are rich green in color and have prominent veins, while many cultivars, such as those in the Crispum Group, produce a fountain of eye-catching frilly-edged leaves. The striped lines of copper-colored spore cases beneath the fronds are another decorative feature. This fern thrives in dappled light; it requires moisture while establishing but then tolerates dry shade when mature.

'Golden Queen' has crimped leaves that are a rich yellow in spring, darkening to green.

MAIDENHAIR SPLEENWORT

ASPLENIUM TRICHOMANES

HEIGHT AND SPREAD 6 × 6 in (15 × 15 cm)
SOIL Moist but well-drained
HARDINESS Fully hardy
SUN ☀ ☀

In its native habitat, this compact evergreen fern grows in the crevices between rocks and the cracks in the trunks of trees, making it the perfect choice for a dry-stone wall. Its rosettes of bright green fronds, made up of small oval segments and set off by near-black stems, create a lacy effect. It will spread to fill any gaps in walls and rockeries, or between paving stones. It needs little aftercare, and tolerates dry soil as well as deep shade once established.

Grow maidenhair spleenwort in a shady rockery or dry-stone wall.

LADY FERN *ATHYRIUM FILIX-FEMINA*

HEIGHT AND SPREAD Up to 4 × 3 ft (120 × 90 cm)
SOIL Moist; neutral to acid
HARDINESS Fully hardy
SUN ☀ ☼

Use this tall deciduous fern to add height and structure to a bed or fernery. In spring, it produces a large clump of fresh green, triangular fronds, with reddish midribs and tooth-edged segments that create a lacy effect. The cultivar *A. filix femina* subsp. *angustum* f. *rubellum* 'Lady in Red' has bright red stems that contrast with the green foliage. Underplant this fern with spring bulbs to inject color into a border before the fronds unfurl, and cut back the old foliage in late winter to make way for new growth.

'Lady in Red' has a delicate form picked out in contrasting reds and greens.

PAINTED LADY FERN *ATHYRIUM NIPONICUM* VAR. *PICTUM*

HEIGHT AND SPREAD Up to 20 × 48 in (50 × 120 cm)
SOIL Moist; neutral to acid
HARDINESS Hardy to 5°F (−15°C)
SUN ☀ ☼

The deciduous painted lady fern, or Japanese painted fern, produces deeply cut gray-green fronds with a silvery sheen, flushed with reddish-purple tones on the stems and midrib area. This versatile plant will be happy in a container or in the ground but needs acidic potting mix or acid soil to thrive. Desirable cultivars include 'Red Beauty' which has vivid burgundy-red stems and midribs on mature fronds, and 'Silver Falls', with its bright silver foliage and dark maroon midribs.

The silvery fronds of this fern create highlights in gloomy areas of the yard.

HARD FERN *BLECHNUM SPICANT*

HEIGHT AND SPREAD 20 × 20 in (50 × 50 cm)
SOIL Moist; neutral to acid
HARDINESS Fully hardy
SUN ☀ ☼

The hard, or deer, fern produces rosettes of evergreen, ladderlike fronds that create a dark green, leafy foil for spring bulbs and other shade-loving flowers. The new growth also makes a beautiful feature when it unfurls. Coping with deep shade, it grows best in moist, neutral to acid soil, or acidic potting mix in a pot. Try planting groups in damp areas of the yard, including those that are prone to waterlogging such as the banks of a natural pond or stream. Remove old or tattered foliage in spring.

The hard fern's new fronds produce a decorative feature when they unfurl in spring.

MALE FERN *DRYOPTERIS FILIX-MAS/D. AFFINIS*

HEIGHT AND SPREAD Up to 4 × 3 ft (1.2 × 1 m)
SOIL Moist but well-drained
HARDINESS Fully hardy
SUN ☀ ☼

The male fern (*Dryopteris filix-mas*) and its close relative the scaly male fern (*D. affinis*) are stately plants that produce a shuttlecock of rich green triangular fronds; those of *D. affinis* are golden green when young and have golden scales on the stems. *D. filix-mas* copes well with dry shade beneath trees and with hot summers, given sufficient shade. The scaly male fern requires a little more moisture, but will also survive short periods of drought. Cut back the old fronds in early spring to make way for new growth.

Dryopteris affinis 'Cristata' produces unusual fronds with crested tips.

COPPER SHIELD FERN *DRYOPTERIS ERYTHROSORA*

HEIGHT AND SPREAD 24 × 20 in (60 × 40 cm)
SOIL Moist
HARDINESS Hardy to 14°F (−10°C)
SUN ☀

Also known as the buckler or autumn fern, this deciduous or semi-evergreen plant forms a compact clump of triangular fronds that unfurl coppery-pink, turning dark green in summer. While it is tolerant of a range of soil conditions, for the best results grow it in moist conditions—mulching with leaf mold will help retain moisture in the soil. The cultivar 'Brilliance' has bright red young fronds. Cut back the old growth in late winter or early spring to make way for new fronds.

The copper shield fern gets its name from the color of the new growth in spring.

WALLICH'S WOOD FERN *DRYOPTERIS WALLICHIANA*

HEIGHT AND SPREAD 3 × 5 ft (0.9 × 1.5 m)
SOIL Well-drained; moist but well-drained
HARDINESS Hardy to 5°F (−15°C)
SUN ☀ ☀

This tough fern makes a lush shuttlecock of tall fronds that are bright yellowish-green when they unfurl in spring and then turn fully green, with blackish-brown scales on the back. Useful for areas under trees, since it tolerates dry shade once established, this deciduous or semi-evergreen fern combines well with other shade-lovers in a woodland setting. Cut back old growth in late winter, especially if growing it with winter bulbs such as snowdrops that make use of the light before the new growth appears.

The hairy stems of this wood fern look pink at the tips when the fronds unfurl in spring.

SHUTTLECOCK FERN *MATTEUCCIA STRUTHIOPTERIS*

HEIGHT AND SPREAD 5 × 2 ft (1.5 × 0.6 m)
SOIL Moist but well-drained; moist
HARDINESS Hardy to 5°F (−15°C)
SUN ☀ ☀

Most striking in spring when the pale green, finely divided fronds unfurl, this deciduous fern forms a large shuttlecock of lacy foliage. It tolerates boggy conditions and looks beautiful planted near water or at the edge of a deciduous tree canopy, where it will make a textured backdrop to more colorful plants that enjoy part shade, such as hardy geraniums and astrantias (see *pp.70 and 68*). Apply a mulch of leaf mold around clumps to help conserve soil moisture and cut back the old fronds in late winter or early spring.

The neat shuttlecock of pale green fronds will light up a gloomy area of the yard.

SENSITIVE FERN *ONOCLEA SENSIBILIS*

HEIGHT AND SPREAD 3 × 6½ ft (1 × 2 m)
SOIL Moist but well-drained; moist; acid
HARDINESS Fully hardy
SUN ☀ ☀

Loved for its large, triangular fronds comprising fingerlike, wavy-edged segments (pinnae), the sensitive fern is bright pinkish-bronze in spring and then matures to pale green as summer progresses. Ideally, grow it in dappled shade close to water or in a border with moist, preferably acid soil, where it will form large clumps. The fronds of this deciduous fern will scorch if exposed to full sun, hence the common name. Cut back old growth in late winter or early spring to make way for new fronds.

The sensitive fern's large fronds are divided into striking, wavy-edged segments.

ROYAL FERN *OSMUNDA REGALIS*

HEIGHT AND SPREAD 8 × 13 ft (2.5 × 4 m)
SOIL Moist but well-drained; moist; acid
HARDINESS Fully hardy
SUN ☀ ☀

The aptly named royal fern is indeed majestic, its large, bright green sterile fronds unfurling in spring to form impressive clumps that turn reddish-bronze in the fall. It also produces rusty-colored fertile fronds that are shorter in length and look like feathery blooms. This deciduous fern prefers moist, acid soil and makes a striking statement planted near a water feature such as a pond or stream. The foliage should be cut back in late winter or in early spring to make way for new growth.

The majestic royal fern needs plenty of space to display its large triangular fronds.

COMMON POLYPODY *POLYPODIUM VULGARE*

HEIGHT AND SPREAD 12 × 36 in (30 × 90 cm)
SOIL Well-drained; moist but well-drained
HARDINESS Fully hardy
SUN ☀ ☀

The perfect choice for a rock garden or wall, the common polypody is an evergreen fern with lance-shaped, deeply divided, dark green fronds. It is an epiphyte, which means it can grow on other plants, and in the wild it is often seen emerging from the fissures in the trunks and branches of deciduous trees. This versatile fern is equally happy in damp or dry soils, and spreads to form large colonies in woodland. It is very easy to maintain; simply remove any dead fronds in spring.

The little evergreen common polypody will quickly establish in the cracks of a dry-stone wall.

HARD SHIELD FERN *POLYSTICHUM ACULEATUM*

HEIGHT AND SPREAD 24 × 36 in (60 × 90 cm)
SOIL Well-drained
HARDINESS Fully hardy
SUN ☀ ☀

Unassuming but tough, this useful evergreen fern forms a shuttlecock of mid-size, divided green fronds that provide year-round interest. Plant it under deciduous trees, where it will cope well with the dry, shady conditions, and combine it with winter- and spring-flowering bulbs such as snowdrops and bluebells that also thrive there—just ensure that each has sufficient space. The hard shield fern needs little maintenance: simply remove old or tattered fronds in early spring and water young plants during dry spells.

The evergreen fronds of the hard shield fern provide year-round interest.

SOFT SHIELD FERN *POLYSTICHUM SETIFERUM*

HEIGHT AND SPREAD 4 × 3 ft (1.2 × 1 m)
SOIL Well-drained
HARDINESS Fully hardy
SUN ☀ ☀

Like the hard shield fern, this tall evergreen plant copes well with the dry soil beneath deciduous trees. The soft, dark green fronds form an upright clump as they unfurl in spring, and then open to create an elegant vase shape. Perfect for any gloomy spot, either in a woodland-type setting or close to a wall or fence, this fern's lacy fronds will provide a lush backdrop for more colorful flowers such as winter- and spring-flowering bulbs and summer perennials. Cut back old or tattered fronds in spring.

The soft shield fern's lacy evergreen fronds brighten up shady areas with dry soil.

PLANTING CHALLENGES

Areas of deep shade present a major challenge for most plants, because without sufficient sunlight their leaves struggle to photosynthesize and produce enough energy to grow. In these situations, you will have to work with the small number of plants that have adapted to the dimness, and if the soil in your yard is dry, too, your choices will be even more limited. However, there are some beauties in this group that are guaranteed to brighten up difficult areas with lush foliage and dainty flowers.

Feathery *Aruncus* flowers mingle with *Rodgersia* and hostas in this moist bed in deep shade.

INTO THE GLOOM

Dark areas that are overshadowed by tall buildings or walls will offer a home to some beautiful shade-loving plants that need moisture to thrive. Many ferns fall into this group, as well as some dramatic perennials with large sculptural foliage, such as goat's beard (*Aruncus*), *Filipendula*, *Rodgersia*, and dark green-leaved hostas. Combine these beauties with structural shrubs that cope with the darkness, including euonymus, camellias, daphnes, and Japanese aralias (*Fatsia japonica*), together with spring bulbs (see pp.76–79) to brighten the garden earlier in the year, and you will wonder why shady gardens are not more sought after.

HIGH AND DRY

The dry soil beneath mature trees or close to a north-facing wall is suitable only for the toughest of the shade-lovers. Surviving on the few beams of light that may filter down through the branches to the woodland floor, they are to be admired for their resilience. However, you will not be able to create a brightly colored flowery border here, since these stalwarts tend to conserve energy by producing small blooms, often in pale shades that allow pollinators to find them in the dimness. Some plants, such as sweet box (*Sarcococca*), mahonias, epimediums, hellebores, and lungwort (*Pulmonaria*), bloom before the trees' leaves unfurl, taking advantage of the extra light at this time of year, while drought-tolerant ferns such as *Dryopteris*, *Polypodium*, and *Polystichum* don't flower at all; they produce spores on fertile fronds that allow them to reproduce in dry conditions.

These adaptations are a gift for the shade gardener, allowing the creation of a lush, leafy tapestry in the most challenging of spaces. Just weave together a selection of the plants listed above and those on pp.118–121 to create a beautiful border.

Flowering in spring, epidediums take advantage of the increased light levels before the tree canopies unfurl.

TOP TIP IF CONGESTED ROOTS CLOSE TO THE SURFACE ARE MAKING IT DIFFICULT TO PLANT UNDER A TREE CANOPY, TRY INSTALLING A RAISED BED 3 FT (1 M) OR MORE AWAY FROM THE TRUNK. FILL WITH SOIL-BASED POTTING MIX AND INCLUDE PLANTS THAT TOLERATE DRY SHADE.

Hellebores and pink-flowered pulmonarias glow out from the gloom beneath shrubs in this shady border.

PLANTS FOR DEEP, DRY SHADE

Areas of deep shade are challenging places for plants, denying them the light they need to photosynthesize, while the dry soil beneath trees can exacerbate the problem, reducing your planting choices even further. However, nature abhors a vacuum and some tough plants have adapted to cope with these difficult situations, a selection of which is included here. A few ferns (see *pp.112–115*) and bulbs (see *pp.76–79*) will also thrive in the gloom, especially under deciduous trees where they can exploit higher light levels in winter and early spring.

JAPANESE ANEMONE *ANEMONE HUPEHENSIS*

HEIGHT AND SPREAD 3 × 2 ft (90 × 60 cm)
SOIL Well-drained; moist but well-drained
HARDINESS Fully hardy
SUN ☼ ☼ ☀

A great choice for a wild or informal garden, this Japanese anemone forms a skirt of lobed green leaves, with tall stems of saucer-shaped pink flowers in late summer and early fall. The blooms are loved by pollinators and this perennial will soon form a large clump; it also spreads rapidly, so be prepared to dig out unwanted growth. While it flowers best in part shade, it does not mind darker areas. *Anemone × hybrida* (see *p.67*) is less invasive, but does not cope as well in deep shade.

Japanese anemones produce pink saucer-shaped flowers in late summer and early fall.

LADY'S MANTLE *ALCHEMILLA MOLLIS*

HEIGHT AND SPREAD Up to 20 × 20 in (50 × 50 cm)
SOIL Well-drained; moist but well-drained
HARDINESS Fully hardy
SUN ☼ ☼ ☀

Grown for its scallop-edged bright green leaves, this perennial will brighten up gloomy beds in summer, when frothy yellow-green flowers appear above the foliage. Lady's mantle looks particularly beautiful after rain, when drops of water collect on the leaves. This little plant will grow almost anywhere, from paving cracks to beds with heavy clay, though it may flower less profusely in deep shade. However, this could be an advantage, since it will limit its tendency to self-seed.

Scalloped leaves and yellow-green flowers will brighten up a dark corner.

SPOTTED LAUREL *AUCUBA JAPONICA*

HEIGHT AND SPREAD Up to 8 × 8 ft (2.5 × 2.5 m)
SOIL Well-drained; moist but well-drained
HARDINESS Hardy to 5°F (–15°C)
SUN ☼ ☀

The spotted laurel is a tough evergreen shrub that produces leathery green leaves embellished with gold spots or splashes. It is dioecious—male and female flowers are on separate plants—and the blooms on both are small and hardly noticeable. However, female varieties will produce bright red berries if a male is close by, adding colorful highlights when they appear in the fall. It is almost maintenance-free—just remove dead, diseased, or wayward stems in early spring.

Female spotted laurel plants produce bright red fall berries amid the gold-spotted evergreen foliage.

DALMATIAN BELLFLOWER
CAMPANULA PORTENSCHLAGIANA

HEIGHT AND SPREAD 6 × 20 in (15 × 50 cm)
SOIL Well-drained
HARDINESS Fully hardy
SUN ☀

Forming a spreading carpet of kidney-shaped overwintering leaves, this diminutive perennial is covered with small funnel-shaped purple flowers throughout the summer. An undemanding plant, it will grow in any crack or crevice in a shady space, and will cope with very low light conditions, although flowering may be reduced in these settings. It is easy to maintain—simply reduce overly long stems in early spring.

Cascading stems of purple flowers make a colorful carpet throughout the summer months.

ALEXANDRIAN LAUREL DANAE RACEMOSA

HEIGHT AND SPREAD 2 × 2 ft (60 × 60 cm)
SOIL Moist but well-drained
HARDINESS Hardy to 5°F (–15°C)
SUN ☼ ☼ ☀

The Alexandrian laurel is in the same plant family as butcher's broom (see p.64) and produces similar leaflike flattened stems called phylloclades, which create an evergreen effect. However, unlike its cousin, this plant is a hermaphrodite and reliably produces bright red berries in the fall. Adapted to low light and well-drained soils, it grows well under trees, and will also benefit from the shelter they offer. It requires little maintenance—just cut old shoots to the ground in spring.

Bright red berries appear on the Alexandrian laurel in the fall, adding to this shade-lover's charms.

JAPANESE SPINDLE EUONYMUS JAPONICUS

HEIGHT AND SPREAD Up to 6½ × 6½ ft (2 × 2 m)
SOIL Well-drained; moist but well-drained
HARDINESS Fully hardy
SUN ☼ ☼ ☀

Almost bulletproof, the leafy Japanese spindle will grow in the most inhospitable conditions, its oval evergreen foliage decorating dry, shady areas of the yard. Many cultivars feature cream- or yellow-edged foliage, which will brighten up beds near deciduous trees, while the plain green types, such 'Green Spire', will not balk at even deeper shade beneath the canopies or beside a north-facing wall. This shrub rarely succumbs to pests or diseases and requires no regular pruning.

Many Japanese spindles sport variegated leaves that retain their color in shady areas.

WOOD SPURGE EUPHORBIA AMYGDALOIDES VAR. ROBBIAE

HEIGHT AND SPREAD 28 × 36 in (70 × 90 cm)
SOIL Well-drained; moist but well-drained
HARDINESS Fully hardy
SUN ☼ ☀

This shade-loving evergreen perennial is perfect for the darkest, driest areas of the garden, where its rosettes of glossy, dark green leaves will provide year-round interest. Sprays of small, lime-green flowers appear in late spring above the foliage. It will spread to form ground cover under trees and beside walls and fences; just be prepared to dig out unwanted growth if it encroaches into areas reserved for other plants. As with all euphorbias, the sap is poisonous, so wear gloves when handling it.

Wood spurge will produce its slim, green leaves and spring flowers in the darkest of spaces.

CRANESBILL *GERANIUM SPECIES*

HEIGHT AND SPREAD Up to 28 × 24 in (70 × 60 cm)
SOIL Well-drained; moist but well-drained
HARDINESS Fully hardy
SUN ☼ ☀

Most cranesbills, or hardy geraniums, tolerate part shade, but a few are adapted to darker conditions. Both *G. phaeum* and the big-root geranium, *G. macrorrhizum*, are good choices for the deep shade and dry soil under trees. *G. nodosum* will grow almost anywhere and flowers well in deep shade but it is invasive and will pop up all over the yard. The wood geranium, *G. sylvaticum*, will also provide a decorative feature in deep shade, but prefers slightly more moisture than the others.

Geranium macrorrhizum flowers come in shades of pink or white and bloom all summer.

STINKING HELLEBORE *HELLEBORUS FOETIDUS*

HEIGHT AND SPREAD Up to 32 × 18 in (80 × 45 cm)
SOIL Moist but well-drained
HARDINESS Fully hardy
SUN ☼ ☀

While most hellebores are happy in part shade, the stinking hellebore is among the best for darker areas under trees. It acquired its rather unfortunate common name because the leaves emit an unpleasant smell when crushed, but this rarely occurs. The dark green divided foliage of this evergreen perennial is accompanied by nodding, purple-edged, pale green flowers, which persist from late winter to mid-spring. For the rest of the year, its foliage creates a sculptural feature.

The stinking hellebore is a beautiful plant for deep shade, with bold, divided foliage.

BIG BLUE LILY-TURF *LIRIOPE MUSCARI*

HEIGHT AND SPREAD 12 × 18 in (30 × 45 cm)
SOIL Moist but well-drained; neutral to acid
HARDINESS Hardy to 5°F (−15°C)
SUN ☼ ☀

Providing a leafy presence throughout the year, this evergreen perennial looks like a grass with its tufts of narrow, dark green foliage. Spikes of small, violet-purple, long-lasting flowers appear in the fall and are followed by black berries as winter approaches. A great little plant for areas under trees, it performs best in neutral or acid soils. Given these conditions, it will soldier on year after year with little maintenance, and makes an excellent partner for dwarf daffodils.

Lily-turf produces grasslike foliage all year round and spikes of purple flowers in the fall.

OREGON GRAPE *MAHONIA × MEDIA*

HEIGHT AND SPREAD 8 × 8 ft (2.5 × 2.5 m)
SOIL Well-drained; moist but well-drained
HARDINESS Hardy to 5°F (−15°C)
SUN ☼ ☼ ☀

Mahonias are large evergreen shrubs and this hybrid is highly ornamental, bearing glossy green, spiny leaves that create a structural feature beneath trees and in other shady spaces. In late winter, long spikes of small, scented, yellow flowers form a bouquet of nectar-rich blooms for early flying pollinators. Blue berries, loved by blackbirds, follow the flowers. This shrub thrives in most soils, including dry, sandy ground. Remove dead or diseased stems in spring after flowering.

'Winter Sun' produces upright sprays of scented yellow flowers in winter and early spring.

HOLLY OLIVE *OSMANTHUS HETEROPHYLLUS*

HEIGHT AND SPREAD Up to 8 × 8 ft (2.5 × 2.5 m)
SOIL Well-drained; moist but well-drained
HARDINESS Fully hardy
SUN ☼ ◐ ●

Often mistaken for a holly, this *Osmanthus* is useful in areas close to trees or other shady settings, where its spiny, often variegated, evergreen foliage will create an eye-catching feature all year round. In summer and fall, small, white, fragrant flowers appear, sometimes followed by blue-black fruits. However, it may be more reluctant to bloom in deep shade. Tolerant of most soils, this shrub requires little maintenance—just prune out dead or wayward stems in mid- or late spring.

The variegated leaves of 'Tricolor' will retain their color if the plant is grown in full shade.

FOAM FLOWER *TIARELLA CORDIFOLIA*

HEIGHT AND SPREAD 12 × 16 in (30 × 40 cm)
SOIL Moist but well-drained
HARDINESS Hardy to 5°F (−15°C)
SUN ◐ ●

The lobed foliage of this semi-evergreen perennial produces a carpet of green leaves that take on bronze tints in fall and winter. Upright spikes of small creamy-white flowers appear in summer like cones of milky foam, hence the common name. Pink-flowered cultivars such as 'Pink Bouquet' are also available. Tolerant of deep shade and dry soil, this little plant is ideal for areas beneath trees or close to a wall or fence. To keep it looking neat, remove dead leaves in spring.

Foam flower is named for its starry white flowers that bloom for many weeks in summer.

DAVID VIBURNUM *VIBURNUM DAVIDII*

HEIGHT AND SPREAD Up to 2 × 4 ft (0.6 × 1.2 m)
SOIL Well-drained; moist but well-drained
HARDINESS Hardy to 5°F (−15°C)
SUN ◐ ●

The dark green, spear-shaped leaves of this compact evergreen shrub feature deep, linear veins that create an interesting textural effect. Flat-topped heads of small white flowers appear in late spring and on female plants they are followed by bright, metallic blue berries if a male is growing close by, as this is a dioecious plant (see Skimmia on p.64). Purchase plants with and without berries in the fall to ensure you buy both types. Prune only to remove dead and diseased growth when you see it.

Metallic blue berries cover the female plants in the fall and last well into winter.

LESSER PERIWINKLE *VINCA MINOR*

HEIGHT AND SPREAD 20 × 36 in (50 × 90 cm)
SOIL Well-drained; moist but well-drained
HARDINESS Fully hardy
SUN ☼ ◐ ●

This evergreen sub-shrub will grow almost anywhere, including areas of deep shade and dry soil beneath trees. It quickly forms a clump of upright stems covered with glossy, green leaves, and the violet-blue flowers appear from spring to late summer. Variegated forms with cream-edged leaves are also available. While it may spread beyond its allocated space in other parts of the yard, its vigor is diminished when it is grown in low light and on poor soils.

The lesser periwinkle will brighten a dark corner with its evergreen foliage and long-lasting violet-blue flowers.

COOL CROPS

When it comes to making a fruit and vegetable patch, many sources will advise you to locate it in a bright, open, sunny spot, but while these conditions will suit the widest range of crops, many can be successfully grown in part shade. However, the choice for full shade is almost zero, so make sure your beds have a few hours of direct sun each day, and consider installing a few raised beds to lift your crops up to reach a little more sunlight.

Drill drainage holes in an old recycled pan to accommodate a few lettuce plants on a cool, shady patio.

SHADY LEAVES

Growing your own vegetables is one of the joys of owning a garden and you do not have to forfeit fresh produce just because your plot is in shade. The list of crops that tolerate low light conditions is quite broad, and includes many leafy vegetables, such as lettuce, kale, green cabbages, Swiss chard, spinach, and bok choy. In fact, lettuces often grow better in some shade, which prevents them from flowering and going to seed too quickly, while the cooler conditions also reduce evaporation rates, keeping the soil moist longer and reducing the need to water your crops as frequently.

Members of the brassica family, including cabbages, kale, and bok choy, are susceptible to attacks by cabbage white butterfly caterpillars, which can decimate crops, so cover them with insect-proof netting to protect them.

Some root vegetables, including carrots and beets, also tolerate part or light shade. Like brassicas, carrots need to be covered with insect-proof netting to protect them from carrot fly. This pest lays its eggs near the plants and the grubs that emerge then tunnel into the roots.

Swiss chard tolerates part shade; both the leaves and the jewel-colored stems are delicious when stir-fried.

SHADE-TOLERANT FRUITS

There are a few woodland plants that will produce a good crop of berries in part shade. Blackberries will deliver a harvest of juicy fruits in a shady corner, particularly if you train the stems on trellis or wires up a wall or fence where the upper stems will receive more light. Small, sweet, wild strawberries, which grow on woodland floors, also tolerate low light conditions. Red and white currants and raspberries will provide a crop, too, if given about four to six hours of direct sun each day in summer.

Blackberry plants can produce heavy crops of sweet fruits when grown in part shade.

CHOOSING HERBS

As well as vegetables and fruits, many herbs will grow in a shady bed. Try mint, parsley, dill, chives, cilantro, and sorrel, which all thrive in part shade, but steer clear of the sun-loving Mediterranean herbs, such as sage, thyme, and rosemary. Exceptions to that rule are oregano and bay, both native to southern Europe, which grow well in part shade—surprisingly, bay can also tolerate quite deep shade.

Growing your herbs in pots will allow you to move them to a brighter spot such as a window ledge, if they are growing tall and leggy in a bid to stretch toward more light.

Confine mint to a pot of its own, and don't plant it in the ground if you want to prevent the rampant spreading roots and stems of this vigorous herb from swamping everything in their path.

Parsley will grow well in a pot on a partly shaded patio or in a window box alongside other herbs.

EASY CROPS FOR SHADE

Leafy green vegetables and fruits adapted to woodland edges are perfect crops to grow in a partly shaded area, together with herbs such as mint and parsley that prefer cooler conditions. As well as the choices outlined here, you could also include the Japanese greens mizuna and mibuna and vegetables in the cabbage family (Brassicaceae), such as kohlrabi, radishes, broccoli, and, of course, cabbages themselves, although all need a minimum of three to six hours of sun per day to thrive.

BEETS *BETA VULGARIS*

HEIGHT AND SPREAD 8 x 8 in (20 x 20 cm)
SOIL Well-drained; moist but well-drained
HARDINESS Fully hardy
SUN ☼ ☀

Beets are a cool-season crop, and grow best in spring and fall when temperatures are around 50°F (16°C). It's also happy in part shade, particularly during the summer when the sun is strong. Sow the seed on a sunny windowsill, then plant out at 4 in (10 cm) intervals in well-drained soil, or slightly closer in a large pot. When watered regularly, the sweet roots are quick to develop and will be ready to harvest when they reach the size of a golf ball. The pink-stemmed green leaves are edible, too.

Beets are best harvested when the roots are about the size of a golf ball or slightly larger.

SWISS CHARD *BETA VULGARIS* SUBSP. *CICLA*

HEIGHT AND SPREAD 18 x 18 in (45 x 45 cm)
SOIL Well-drained; moist but well-drained
HARDINESS Fully hardy
SUN ☼ ☀

This colorful leafy vegetable is delicious stir-fried, steamed, or included in salads. It will cope with part shade but the seed is best started off in spring on a sunny windowsill to encourage germination and early growth. When large enough to handle, plant the seedlings out at 12 in (30 cm) intervals in fertile, free-draining soil. You can harvest the leaves when plants are around 4 in (10 cm) for salads, or allow them to mature to their full height and pick individual leaves for cooking as needed. The stems are edible, too.

The colorful stems of Swiss chard are edible and help brighten a bed in part shade.

KALE *BRASSICA OLERACEA* (ACEPHALA GROUP)

HEIGHT AND SPREAD Up to 36 x 36 in (90 x 90 cm)
SOIL Well-drained; moist but well-drained
HARDINESS Fully hardy
SUN ☼ ☀

Easier to grow than some of its cabbage cousins, kale offers a long harvest of green or purple leaves in the fall and winter. Sow seeds under cover or in the garden in spring and, once germinated, space seedlings 20 in (50 cm) apart. Cover crops with insect-proof netting to guard against flea beetle and cabbage white butterflies. Keep well watered and harvest the leaves regularly to encourage a continuous crop. Young plants can be used for salads, or allow them to mature for a leafy cooked vegetable.

Curly kale's vitamin-rich dark green leaves can be harvested from fall through winter.

BOK CHOY *BRASSICA RAPA* SUBSP. *CHINENSIS*

HEIGHT AND SPREAD Up to 12 × 12 in (30 × 30 cm)
SOIL Moist but well-drained
HARDINESS Fully hardy
SUN ☼

This fast-maturing Asian brassica can be used in salads and steamed or stir-fried. It likes cool, damp conditions and grows best in light shade, especially in summer. Sow seeds on a windowsill from early spring and plant out at 8–12 in (20–30 cm) spacings in the ground or large pots. Keep well watered—dry soil may prompt early flowering (bolting) and cover with netting (see Kale). Use young leaves for salads, or wait until plants develop full-size heads for cooking, which will be 8–10 weeks after sowing.

'White Stem' is a decorative bok choy with creamy-white stems and tender green leaves.

CARROTS (BABY) *DAUCUS CAROTA* SUBSP. *SATIVUS*

HEIGHT AND SPREAD 18 × 18 in (45 × 45 cm)
SOIL Moist but well-drained; moist
HARDINESS Fully hardy
SUN ☼ ☼

A staple for many meals, these roots are happy with afternoon shade, especially during the summer months when hot sun can dry out the soil. Sow seeds in shallow drills in situ from early spring, then be patient, since carrots are slow to germinate. Pull out young seedlings or nip the top growth off older ones to the spacings given on the packet. Cover with fleece to prevent carrot fly laying eggs near your crops, and water sparingly during dry spells. Harvest when the roots reach the desired size.

Carrots can be red or purple as well as orange, and all grow well in afternoon shade.

LETTUCE *LACTUCA SATIVA*

HEIGHT AND SPREAD Up to 8 × 8 in (20 × 20 cm)
SOIL Moist but well-drained; moist
HARDINESS Hardy to 28°F (−2°C)
SUN ☼

This fast-maturing leafy salad crop is easy to grow in the ground or in peat-free potting mix and will be very happy in part shade, where the cooler conditions will help prevent early flowering (bolting) in summer. Buy loose leaf cut-and-come-again types for baby leaves or opt for lettuces such as romaine that form a large, firm head. Sow batches of seeds thinly at intervals from early spring to provide a continuous crop—they won't germinate if temperatures are too high. Keep crops well watered.

Grow an assortment of lettuce varieties to add color and texture to your salad dishes.

SPINACH *SPINACIA OLERACEA*

HEIGHT AND SPREAD Up to 18 × 18 in (45 × 45 cm)
SOIL Moist but well-drained
HARDINESS Some varieties hardy to 14°F (−10°C)
SUN ☼ ☼

These nutritious leaves are delicious in salads or steamed or stir-fried for cooked dishes. Spinach needs sun if grown in spring or fall but prefers part shade in summer, which helps protect this cool-season crop from bolting (flowering prematurely) in hot, dry weather. Sow seeds in batches from early to late spring in fertile soil or large pots of peat-free potting mix, and thin to the spacings recommended on the packet. Water regularly and protect plants from slugs and snails.

Spinach leaves are packed with nutrients and grow well in large pots in light shade.

ALPINE STRAWBERRY *FRAGARIA VESCA*

HEIGHT AND SPREAD Up to 8 × 8 in (20 × 20 cm)
SOIL Moist but well-drained
HARDINESS Fully hardy
SUN ☼ ☀

Also known as woodland strawberries, these plants thrive in semi-shaded areas and produce a succession of small, sweet fruits throughout summer. They need little attention apart from watering during dry spells while they are establishing. These little plants will self-seed, providing you with more fruit the following year—they don't produce runners like the larger strawberry varieties. Use them to edge a bed or border or plant them in a container of peat-free, loam-based potting mix.

Growing wild on woodland edges, this little strawberry is one of the easiest fruits to grow.

RED AND WHITE CURRANTS *RIBES RUBRUM*

HEIGHT AND SPREAD Up to 6½ × 3 ft (2 × 1 m)
SOIL Well-drained; moist but well-drained
HARDINESS Fully hardy
SUN ☼ ☀

These currants add a sharp, sweet flavor to desserts, while the tall shrubs lend a colorful note to productive gardens. Plant in the ground or in large pots of peat-free loam-based potting mix in a sheltered spot. They can be grown as free-standing bushes, but training the stems on wires or trellis on a wall or fence ensures the currants receive more light. Keep plants in pots well watered—those in the ground will rarely need watering once established. In early spring, apply a high potash fertilizer.

White and red currants are best trained on wires or a trellis when grown in part shade.

BLACKBERRY *RUBUS FRUTICOSUS*

HEIGHT AND SPREAD Up to 6½ × 6½ ft (2 × 2 m)
SOIL Moist but well-drained
HARDINESS Fully hardy
SUN ☀

Cultivated forms of the brambles you see growing in woodlands are perfect for shady yards. Opt for a thornless cultivar to make harvesting the berries easier, and choose a sheltered site with moisture-retentive but free-draining soil; established plants will tolerate periods of drought. Train the stems on sturdy wires or supports to allow good air flow and sufficient light to reach the fruits. Old growth is usually removed after fruiting in the fall, but check your cultivar for its pruning needs.

'Chester' is thornless and produces heavy crops of large, sweet fruits in late summer.

RASPBERRY *RUBUS IDAEUS*

HEIGHT AND SPREAD Up to 6½ × 6½ ft (2 × 2 m)
SOIL Moist but well-drained
HARDINESS Fully hardy
SUN ☼ ☀

Raspberries will fruit in light shade, but may bear a smaller crop than those grown in full sun. Choose from summer- or fall-fruiting varieties, or buy both for a long harvest. Select a sheltered area, out of winds that may damage the thin fruiting stems, and erect a system of posts and horizontal wires to tie the stems to, ideally set out in rows running north to south so the plants won't shade each other too much. Cover plants with bird-proof netting, and check your particular cultivar for its pruning needs.

Fall-fruiting canes are pruned to the ground in late winter to promote new growth.

CILANTRO *CORIANDRUM SATIVUM*

HEIGHT AND SPREAD Up to 20 × 12 in (50 × 30 cm)
SOIL Well-drained; moist but well-drained
HARDINESS Hardy to 34°F (1°C)
SUN ☼ ☼

Grown for its edible leaves and seeds, this annual herb is native to southern Europe and the Middle East. While happy in sun, it will produce its citrus-flavored foliage longer when grown in some shade, which delays flowering. Sow seeds in pots indoors in spring and plant out seedlings after the frosts have passed, in the ground or in containers of peat-free multipurpose potting mix. Sowing in batches every two weeks will give you a continuous crop throughout summer. Keep moist but avoid overwatering.

Growing cilantro in part shade delays flowering and prolongs leaf growth.

MINT *MENTHA*

HEIGHT AND SPREAD 20 × 36 in (50 × 90 cm)
SOIL Moist but well-drained
HARDINESS Hardy to 5°F (−15°C)
SUN ☼

An aromatic perennial herb, mint can be used to make tea or included in many dishes. Most common types grow well in part shade, except for the variegated pineapple mint, *Mentha suaveolens* 'Variegata', which prefers brighter conditions. All should be grown in a pot of peat-free loam-based potting mix, where their root systems cannot run riot through the garden. Keep well watered in dry spells and cut back after flowering to promote more leafy stems. Feed in spring with a fertilizer designed for leafy crops.

Loved for its fresh flavor, this perennial herb is easy to grow in a large pot in part shade.

SWEET CICELY *MYRRHIS ODORATA*

HEIGHT AND SPREAD Up to 4 × 3 ft (1.2 × 1 m)
SOIL Moist but well-drained
HARDINESS Hardy to 5°F (−15°C)
SUN ☼

Not grown as widely as it deserves, this large, handsome perennial herb doubles as a beautiful leafy border plant for an area in part shade. Its aniseed-flavored, bright green, ferny leaves can be used in salads or to sweeten rhubarb and other acidic fruits. The foliage is accompanied by flat heads of tiny white flowers in spring, followed by slim, upright seed heads, which also taste of aniseed. It is easy to grow— simply water plants until they are established and it should then take care of itself.

Sweet cicely produces edible aniseed-flavored leaves, flowers, and seed heads.

PARSLEY *PETROSELINUM CRISPUM*

HEIGHT AND SPREAD Up to 20 × 12 in (50 × 30 cm)
SOIL Moist but well-drained
HARDINESS Fully hardy
SUN ☼ ☼

Both flat- and curly-leaved parsley grow well in part shade. This is a biennial plant, which means its foliage grows in the first year and it then flowers in the second year, so it is usually best to grow it from seed each year for the leaves. Sow parsley in pots on a sunny windowsill and when the seedlings are large enough to handle, transplant them to moist but well-drained soil in the ground or a pot of peat-free potting mix. Keep plants well watered and harvest the leaves as needed.

Parsley grows best in well-drained soil that is kept moist but not waterlogged.

Keeping your yard free of weeds prevents them from competing with your plants for water and nutrients.

MAINTAINING SHADY YARDS

All yards require maintenance and you will have to tend your shady space from time to time to keep it looking its best. Young and new plants, and all those in pots, require regular watering, while removing the weeds from your plot will give your ornamentals and crops the space they need to thrive. Pruning can be especially important in a shady yard if shrubs and trees threaten to take even more of the light, while cleaning slippery moss and algae from paths and patios will make them sparkle and prevent accidents.

WATERING AND FEEDING SHADE-LOVERS

The soil in shade tends to dry out slowly, so plants tend to need watering less often than in brighter areas, and if you choose the right plants for your plot, they may survive on rainfall alone once established. However, you will still have to water crops, new plants, and those growing in pots. While mature plants in beds and borders rarely require additional fertilizer, potted plants will need feeding regularly as well.

Water plants and crops early in the morning or in the evening, when evaporation rates are lowest.

MULCHING MATTERS

Choosing the right plants for your site and soil is crucial if you want to reduce the burden of watering once they are established. You can also make life easier by using organic mulches around your plants to trap moisture in the soil. Simply spread a 2-in (5-cm) layer of well-rotted garden compost, manure, or leaf mold over the soil around your plants to form a protective barrier that will help reduce evaporation rates and keep roots hydrated for longer. Trees are best mulched with shredded bark.

Organic mulches also help improve the structure of the soil, creating a better growing environment for your plants. The materials are taken down into the soil by worms, where they help improve the drainage of heavy clay soils and enable free-draining sandy soils to retain more water and nutrients. Apply a mulch every year in spring or fall after heavy rainfall has saturated the soil, leaving a gap around the woody stems of shrubs and trees.

Applying a mulch of organic matter around plants reduces their watering needs by locking moisture in the soil.

DRIP FEED

Once you have planted a new bed or fruit and vegetable plot, your young plants will need irrigating regularly until their roots are well established. The most economical and eco-friendly way to water them is with a seep or drip hose, which slowly releases water into the soil with little or no wastage. Attach the hose to an outdoor faucet or a rain barrel and lay it around your plants, then cover it with a mulch. Installing a programmable timer that automatically irrigates your plants at preset times is a good idea if you don't have time to water manually.

A drip hose laid close to young plants and crops will deliver water to the roots with very little wastage.

Carefully measure out the recommended dose of liquid fertilizer to avoid overfeeding your plants.

FOOD FOR THOUGHT

Research by the Royal Horticultural Society in the UK shows that most soils contain sufficient nutrients for good plant growth, so you probably will not need to fertilize beds and borders. In fact, overfeeding can lead to pollution when excess nitrates filter into the groundwater, which then flows to rivers and oceans. However, some crops may need fertilizing, especially those that produce fruit. Natural fertilizers such as those containing seaweed extract will usually suffice.

Potted plants will also need regular applications of fertilizer once the food in the potting mix has run out, usually about six weeks after planting. For permanent perennials, shrubs, and trees, you can apply a slow-release fertilizer such as bonemeal in spring, or a balanced liquid fertilizer such as seaweed extract at regular intervals throughout the growing season from spring to late summer. When applying a slow-release product, carefully remove a little potting mix from the top of the pot and replace it with fresh potting mix combined with the fertilizer.

Potted annual plants such as summer bedding will need topping up with potassium-rich liquid fertilizer if they start to flag in summer. Avoid the leaves and flowers when applying, and do not exceed the recommended dose. Plants do not need feeding during the winter months when they are dormant.

WATERING PLANTS IN POTS

All plants in containers will need regular watering, since their roots cannot tap into supplies deep in the ground like those growing in the soil. Ensure your pots have drainage holes in the bottom to prevent waterlogging and water them every few days when the weather warms up. Each time you water, give your plants a long drink so the potting mix is completely saturated—stop when you see it coming out of the drainage holes at the bottom. You can install an automatic watering system, too, or add self-watering bulbs and globes that will irrigate your plants for short periods, such as while you're on vacation.

Target water onto the soil when irrigating plants in pots to ensure it reaches the roots.

WEEDING SOLUTIONS

The low light levels in shady sites slow plant growth, which can be a blessing since it means that many weeds will fail to germinate and grow in these areas. However, a few woodlanders will take root and spread unless they are kept in check. Getting to know those most likely to colonize your shady spaces will allow you to remove them before they cause problems—but avoid using chemical herbicides that can harm beneficial insects and the environment.

Carefully dig out the whole root system of perennial weeds such as ground elder to prevent them regrowing.

Herb robert may be considered a weed, but its pretty pink flowers attract pollinators and it's easy to remove.

WHAT IS A WEED?

A common description of a weed is simply a plant in the wrong place, although rampant plants such as hedge bindweed are rarely welcome in any garden. Other shade-lovers, such as the decorative annual herb robert (*Geranium robertianum*) and perennial lesser celandine (*Ficaria verna*), are less invasive and you may wish to tolerate small patches, since they provide food for beneficial insects and are quite easy to pull out if they become a nuisance. Nettles are not as easy to eradicate but they, too, support a range of wildlife, including some butterflies and seed-eating birds. You can also use them to make teas or add to soups. So, while you may not want nettles swamping a flowerbed, consider allowing a few to grow in a quiet area of the yard.

KEEPING WEEDS AT BAY

One of the easiest ways to minimize weed numbers in your garden is to fill all open areas of soil with the plants you love. This will provide few gaps for seeds to settle and germinate, and even shade-tolerant weeds will struggle to grow under a dense canopy of foliage.

Also familiarize yourself with the seedlings of common weeds that pop up in your garden and keep watch for them in spring. You can then dig them out of the soil by hand or hoe off annuals and seedlings. Roots of pernicious weeds such as bindweed and ground elder will need to be removed carefully, since any root left will develop into a new plant.

Push a Dutch hoe through the soil just under the surface to sever weeds' roots from their stems.

SIX SHADE-LOVING WEEDS

Ground elder (*Aegopodium podagraria*) This fast-growing perennial weed will quickly swamp its neighbors with a blanket of green foliage with spear-shaped leaflets. Rounded domes of white flowers appear in summer. Dig out the whole plant, including all the roots, and keep checking for regrowth, removing it as soon as you see it.

Rosebay willowherb (*Chamaenerion angustifolium*) A tall shade-tolerant woodlander, rosebay willowherb produces tall spires of pretty nectar-rich pink flowers, loved by pollinators. However, it can quickly overwhelm a small space, spreading via underground stems and seeds. Dig it out and check for new seedlings in the spring.

Hedge bindweed (*Calystegia sepium*) This rampant climber will happily grow in shade, its twining stems soon strangling surrounding plants and swamping them beneath its heart-shaped leaves and white trumpet-like flowers. Dig it out as best you can, and continue to remove any new growth as soon as you see it to keep this weed in check.

Enchanter's nightshade (*Circaea lutetiana*) A common plant in woodlands and shady borders, this perennial thrives in moist soils. It produces heart-shaped leaves and upright stems of tiny white flowers. It spreads via copious seeds and underground stems (rhizomes), but it is easy to pull or dig out when young, so keep an eye out for the seedlings.

Herb bennet (*Geum urbanum*) Also known as wood avens, this prolific self-seeding perennial loves damp, shady sites and produces divided green leaves and tiny buttercup-like flowers. It spreads via root fragments and seeds and can be eradicated by hoeing the seedlings in spring or digging out mature plants later in the year, ideally before they set seed.

Docks (*Rumex* species) This perennial weed produces large spear-shaped leaves and tall, rusty-colored seed heads. The long tap root makes it difficult to control, since it will regrow from the tip if you don't dig it out. However, removing at least 5–6 in (12–15 cm) of the root often restricts regrowth. Also look out for young plants, which are easier to remove.

PRUNING TIPS

Choosing shrubs and trees that suit your yard's size and light levels should minimize the need to prune them, though some can be cut regularly to produce more flowering stems or simply to keep them in shape. Learning when and how to prune your plants will ensure they remain healthy, and there are some general rules you can follow, but some have individual pruning needs, so look them up before you start.

Use a clean, sharp pruning saw or loppers to cut wide branches that are thicker than a pencil.

WHEN TO PRUNE

Most deciduous trees are pruned when they are dormant, from early winter to early spring, but members of the *Prunus* genus, including cherries and plums, should be pruned in summer. These trees are prone to the fungal disease silver leaf and to bacterial cankers, which are more prevalent in fall and winter. Evergreen trees such as hollies are pruned in late spring, while conifers are best cut from mid-spring to midsummer.

Spring- and winter-flowering shrubs such as mahonias, witch hazels (*Hamamelis*), and Mexican orange blossom (*Choisya*) are pruned after flowering in spring or early summer. These plants flower on stems produced the year before they flower. Those that bloom later in the year, such as *Hydrangea paniculata* and *Hypericum*, should be cut earlier in spring, as they develop flowers on stems that are produced in the same year. Mophead hydrangeas (*H. macrophylla*), while flowering in summer, are an exception to this rule, and should be pruned lightly in mid-spring.

Prune mophead hydrangeas in mid-spring, taking stems down to the first or second healthy bud from the tip.

Make a straight cut across a stem above opposite buds.

Make a slanting cut just above a bud on plants with stems arranged alternately.

SIMPLE PRUNING CUTS

When cutting plants, make sure you have the appropriate tools and that they are sharp and clean. Cut just above a bud (slight swelling, bump, or darker line on the stem) or side stem. Where the buds are arranged in opposite pairs, make a straight cut just above them; for plants with buds arranged alternately along the stem, cut at an angle above a bud, so rain will drain away from it, thereby preventing rot. Do not prune too close to a bud, which may damage it, and don't cut a stem between buds, since this may cause the wood above the lower bud to die back.

REMOVING TREE BRANCHES

When removing a heavy tree branch, cut it in stages to prevent it tearing and ripping bark off the trunk, which will open the plant up to infection. Make the final cut at an angle just beyond the crease in the bark, where the branch emerges from the trunk, leaving a small stub. Do not cut flush with the trunk as this may injure the phloem, which is just beneath the surface and transports sugars around the tree. This method also leaves the tree's healing tissue intact, and the wound will soon be covered by a layer of protective bark.

Make a cut just beyond the crease in the bark on a tree trunk to leave the healing tissue here intact.

EXPERT HELP

Scaling a ladder to prune a tree can be very dangerous, so cut only branches and stems that are easy to reach, and leave pruning above head height and major restorative work to the experts. Call in a tree surgeon or an arborist, checking first that they are a member of a professional organization and insured before you hire them. Also ask how they will be removing the pruned wood—if you have no side access, it may have to come through your house, so you will need to move items and protect the flooring to avoid any damage.

EASY COPPICING

A few shade-loving trees and shrubs, including field maples (*Acer campestre*), hazels (*Corylus avellana*), and redbuds (*Cercis canadensis*), lend themselves to a pruning technique known as coppicing. This is where all the stems are cut to the ground, stimulating new growth from the base. It can be used to renovate old plants or to create a multi-stemmed effect, while also limiting the height of large trees, which can be a benefit if a mature plant would cast more shade.

Leave plants unpruned until they are a couple years old and have established a good root system. Then, in late winter or early spring, cut all growth to about 4 in (10 cm) from the ground. The following year, shorten the stems that develop back to 3 in (8 cm) from the ground, before the buds open, and in subsequent years, cut back to the previous year's stubs. You may also have to cut out crossing stems if growth is too congested.

Use a professional tree surgeon to renovate a tree or undertake pruning above head height.

Cutting stems almost down to the ground stimulates fresh new growth while limiting a tree's height.

CLEANING A SHADY YARD

Features such as paths and patios are prone to moss, algae, and lichen growth in shady sites, making them slippery and hazardous, but cleaning them regularly will help keep them safe and looking good. Wooden and metal furniture can also weather quickly in damp, shady spaces, so take action to prevent it from deteriorating. Just avoid harsh detergents that can pollute water features and groundwater.

Metal furniture is prone to rusting in cool, shady spaces, but it can be revitalized with some special paint.

Power washing a timber deck will quickly remove slippery algae, lichens, and moss from the surface.

MAINTAINING PATIOS AND DECKS

Shady paths, paved seating areas, and timber decks often turn green in winter, when damp conditions promote the growth of algae, lichens, and moss. While these do not damage the hard landscaping materials, they can make them slippery and dangerous. Although you may be able to alleviate the problem by pruning overhanging shrubs and trees to allow more sunlight through to dry the surfaces quickly, they will probably still require cleaning each spring.

Power washing these surfaces is the easiest and most efficient way to remove algae and moss. Wear goggles when using a power washer and be prepared to get wet, as the dirty water is prone to splashing up. The only drawback is that these machines use large volumes of water and can cause temporary flooding, so if this is a problem in your yard, try using a stiff brush and an ordinary garden hose to clean the surface instead.

Never use detergents or harsh chemicals near planting or water features as they will pollute the groundwater and can cause algal blooms in ponds. Most dirt will be removed by water alone.

Throughout the warmer months, brush the surfaces with a stiff broom, which will help keep them free from green, slippery growths and debris.

Apply an eco-friendly wood stain to softwood furniture to maintain the color and prevent it from rotting.

CARING FOR WOODEN FURNITURE

Plastic furniture, including sofas and chairs made from artificial woven rattan, can be cleaned easily with water and a soft, damp cloth, but wooden pieces on shady, damp patios may develop lichens and algae growths, and they can also deteriorate faster than in sunny areas.

Hardwood lawn furniture is more resilient to weathering than untreated softwood, but make sure the legs of all timber pieces are set on a solid surface that dries quickly after rain, rather than damp soil or grass, which will soon cause them to rot.

Hardwood furniture just needs brushing with warm water—use a gentle soap product on stubborn stains, but ensure the dirty water does not drain into a pond, if you have one. Over time, hardwood weathers to a natural silvery gray color unless you apply a UV protection cleaner or wood stain.

To keep softwood pieces clean, lightly sand furniture that has ingrained algae and lichens or brush it down and wash with water and a lint-free cloth. Leave to dry before applying an eco-friendly wood stain or paint containing preservative. You will need to repeat this process every year to maintain the color and prevent your furniture from rotting.

TOP TIP LICHEN AND MOSS CAN CREATE A BEAUTIFUL PATINA ON BACKYARD FEATURES SUCH AS POTS AND SCULPTURE, LENDING AN AGED, WEATHERED LOOK TO THE SPACE, SO LEAVE THEM BE IF YOU WANT TO CREATE THIS EFFECT AND SAVE TIME CLEANING THEM.

RUST REMOVAL

Metal furniture, unless it is powder coated or made from stainless steel or aluminum, will rust when left outside in the yard, potentially causing irreversible damage, and staining clothing if seats are affected. Check items regularly for signs of rust and remove it with a metal brush before applying a metal paint designed for external use. Repainting your pieces every couple of years should keep them looking good. Remember to also oil hinges, fixings, and brackets.

Remove rust from metal furniture with a wire brush and repaint it very couple of years to prevent further damage.

SHADY YARD PROBLEM-SOLVER

Growing plants in the conditions they enjoy can reduce the risk of diseases taking hold, but problems may still occur, especially in cold, damp areas or during prolonged periods of drought. To minimize the incidence of diseases attacking your plants, avoid planting in areas prone to waterlogging; the dry soils beneath trees; or close to large evergreens, walls, and fences. Also act quickly if you spot any problems.

Plants adapted to your shady site and soil conditions will be less likely to succumb to diseases.

CAREFUL CHOICES

The cool, damp conditions that often prevail in shady sites can provide a breeding ground for some plant fungal diseases. Equally, plants that are stressed because the soil is too dry may also succumb to infection. While selecting plants adapted to these conditions can help prevent disease, it's always a good idea to know what the symptoms are in case yours come under attack.

When assessing an ailing plant, first rule out dehydration. Dry soil will cause plants to wilt, while the leaves may also turn yellow and fall, since a lack of water prevents roots from taking up nutrients. A long drink will solve the problem, but you may also want to consider moving plants that are not adapted to drought if the site is prone to drying out.

Wilting plants, particularly if they are young, may just need a long drink to revive them.

> **TOP TIP** DECIDUOUS HEDGES CAN REDUCE WIND SPEEDS IN EXPOSED SHADY SPACES, PROVIDING A SHELTER BELT WHERE A WIDER SELECTION OF PLANTS WILL THRIVE, WHILE OFFERING A HABITAT FOR WILDLIFE.

DEALING WITH DISEASES

A common fungal disease that often affects plants growing in dry soils is powdery mildew, which causes a white, powdery growth on the leaves, flowers, and fruits, and, in severe cases, distorted growth. Remove infected parts and improve the air flow between plants by spacing them more widely and pruning congested stems. Avoid planting in sheltered areas close to walls or fences, or directly under mature trees, and don't apply nitrogen-rich fertilizers that promote soft, succulent growth, which is particularly susceptible to this disease. Applying a mulch (see p.130) to lock moisture in the soil will help, too.

Downy mildew is another widespread fungal disease, but this one takes hold in damp conditions. It causes discoloration of the upper leaf surfaces and a white, gray, or purple mold below. The foliage may then turn brown or yellow and fall in some species, such as tobacco plants (*Nicotiana*) and busy lizzies (*Impatiens*). Pick off the affected leaves and remove badly infected plants (do not compost). To prevent further outbreaks, avoid overhead watering, since wet leaves are prone to the disease, and irrigate in the morning so any damp foliage has time to dry out during the day. Spacing plants out to improve the air flow between them will also help.

Phytophthora root rot and other types of rot are likely to occur on plants growing on waterlogged soils. Wilting, yellow leaves and dead stems are among the symptoms, while the leaves of conifers turn gray. Beneath the surface, the roots will have rotted away and any that remain will be black. Where root rots have taken hold, remove and destroy affected plants by placing them in a bag and putting them in the trash. Also replace the soil around the roots with fresh topsoil.

The risk of these potentially fatal diseases can be minimized by improving the soil drainage. Use a fork to break up compacted pans of heavy clay soil that may be inhibiting water flow, or consider installing drains. Applying mulches each year may also improve conditions. Alternatively, you can embrace areas prone to flooding by planting bog plants that are adapted to wet soils and resistant to these types of rot.

Camellias are hardy but morning sun on frosted plants can kill the flowers, so avoid planting them in east-facing sites.

FOCUS ON FROST

Damage from frost can be exacerbated in shady spaces, where it will remain longer than in sunny sites. "Frost pockets" often develop in dips and valleys, since cold air travels downhill and settles in these spots. If your garden is in a frost pocket, select fully hardy plants, which will not be affected by the cold, and cover new or young plants that are susceptible to damage with garden fleece. You could also plant a hedge farther up the hillside, which will trap the frost behind it and protect the garden below. However, hedges can create frost pockets of their own on the uphill side, so if your plot is on a slope with a hedge along the bottom, remove some of the lower stems to allow the cold air to pass through it to the valley below.

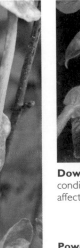

Downy mildew is exacerbated by damp conditions and causes discoloration of the affected leaves.

Powdery mildew affects plants that are growing on dry soils, and causes white, powdery growths.

INDEX

Page numbers in **bold** refer to main entries.

Author Zia Allaway

AUTHOR'S ACKNOWLEDGMENTS

Many thanks to Marek Walisiewicz at Cobalt id for commissioning me to write this book and to Paul Reid for his beautiful designs. Thanks also to editor Diana Vowles, and to the team at Dorling Kindersley for their help in fine-tuning the words.

PUBLISHER'S ACKNOWLEDGMENTS

DK would like to thank Mary-Clare Jerram for developing the original concept; Vanessa Bird for indexing; Kirsty Seymour-Ure for proofreading; and Paul Reid, Marek Walisiewicz, and the Cobalt team for their hard work in putting this book together.

PICTURE CREDITS

The publisher would like to thank the following for their kind permission to reproduce their photographs:

Alamy Stock Photo: A Garden 30c; A.D.Fletcher 87tl; adrian davies 68tl, 139tr; Adrian Sherratt 22cr; Alexey Ivanov 14bc; Andreas von Einsiedel 42bc, 137br; Andrew Kearton 46bl; Andrew Lawson Photography 95bl; andy lane 70bl; AngieC 68br; Anna Pismenskova 65bc; Anna Stowe Botanica 13bl, 38tr; annmarie finn 38bl; Archive PL 40bl; Arterra Picture Library 72tl, 79tr, 133tl, 133bc; Avalon.red 15c, 76bl, 87bl, 92tl; AY Images 126tr; blickwinkel 12bc, 32tr, 41br, 50tr, 62tl, 63bc, 107br, 115br, 126cl, 126bl; Botanic World 113tl; Botany vision 73tr, 106br, 116cl, 121tc; Cheryl Fleishman 39tr; Christopher Nicholson 19br; Clare Gainey 80cl, 105br, 106cl; csimagebase 81tl; Cyrille REDOR 105tc; Dave Bevan 73br; David Winger 119cl; davidd 84tr; Deborah Vernon 85tr, 122tr; Derek Harris 44tr, 108br; Dorling Kindersley ltd 51tr; Elizabeth Whiting & Associates 13br, 100cl; Ellen Rooney 2c, 36br, 56bl, 138tr; Ernie Janes 74tr, 108tc; Florapix 64tl, 93bl; Flowerphoto 59bl; flowerphotos 32bc, 53br, 127bl; Francisco Martinez 136tr; Frank Hecker 133tc; Gary K Smith 118tr; GC Stock 78br; George Ostertag 112tr; gerard ferry 107bl; Gina Kelly 18br; GKSFlorapics 58bl, 86tl; GREG RYAN 6c; Holmes Garden Photos 65tc, 86bl; Ian Lamond 42tr; Ian Shaw 124bl; ian west 114tl; idp yorkshire collection 10tr; Imagebroker 103br; imageBROKER.com GmbH & Co. KG 123bl; inga spence 122bc; Inna Kozhina 135bl; James Allan 43tl, 72tr; Jason Smalley Photography 36tr, 95tr; jlf06 96tr; joan gravell 67tc; John Gollop 80br; John Martin 51tl, 95br, 109tc, 114tr; John Richmond 19tl, 26br, 58br, 59tl, 60br, 76br, 82tr; Julie Fryer pics 11tr, 96bl, 125bl; Kari Nilsen 11bl; katewarn images 53bl; Kay Roxby 132tr; keith burdett 133bl; Kiki Streitberger 106cr; Klemmitch 8bl; Konrad Zelazowski 71br; Linda Kennedy 55tl, 106bc; Lois GoBe 81br; Lucas Luman Mancheski 97bl; Maria Janicki 124br; mark saunders 18cl; Martin Hughes-Jones 68tr, 93tr, 121bc; Matthew Bruce 16cl, 37tc, 111c; Matthew Noble Horticultural 23c; Matthew Taylor 8c, 52bl, 67bc, 95tl; McPhoto/Rolf Mueller 61tr; MichaelGrant 112br; Mr. Megapixel 63tc; N/A 44c, 45bl; Nadya So 138bl; Nature Photographers Ltd 115tr; NICOLE CUBBIDGE 13bc; Nigel Cattlin 61br, 75bl, 132cl, 139bc; nigel dodds 65tr; nigel FRANCIS 17tl; Nikolay Malshakov 131tc; Olga Miltsova 130tr; P Tomlins 67br; Panther Media GmbH 11cr, 80tr; Paul Maguire 56cr; paul weston 112bl; Philip Pickin 35bl; Photimageon 12tr; Phouy Sondala 127tc; Plantography 71tr; pqpictures.co.uk 61cl; practicalpictures.com 109bc; Prettyawesome 8-9c; Rex May 17br; RM Floral 14cl, 27c, 41tr, 52cr, 73tc, 92bl, 110bl, 116br, 117c, 119bc; Ron Javorsky 51bl; Ros Drinkwater 4-5c; RossHelen editorial 131bl; Roswitha Irmer 13tr; Sabena Jane Blackbird 46br; SASko 134tr; Selfwood 46bl; Sergey Kalyakin 66tr; shapencolour 41tl; Steffen Hauser / botanikfoto 39bl, 47cl, 55tr, 64br, 65br, 103bc; Steve Taylor ARPS 47tr; stivog 22cl; STUDIO75 133br; Tamara Kulikova 107cr; Terry Donnelly 13tc; thrillerfillerspiller 62br, 102tr; Tim Gainey 50b, 54tr, 87br, 126br; Universal Images Group North America LLC / DeAgostini 87tr; V Pikouli 54br; Victority 124tr; Vstock 26cl; Wendy Johnson 53tr; Wiert Nieuman 66br, 119cr; WILDLIFE GmbH 107cl; Wirestock, Inc. 103tr; Wojciech Kozielczyk 136c, 137tl; yanadjana 123tr; Zena Elea 13tl; Zoltan Bagosi 86tr; Zoonar GmbH 45tr, 127br.

Dorling Kindersley: 123RF.com: Taina Sohlman / taina 24tr; Alan Buckingham 134bc, 139bl; Brian North / RHS Chelsea Flower Show 2009 22bc, 33bl; Brian North / RHS Chelsea Flower Show 2010 34tr; Brian North / RHS Hampton Court Flower Show 2010 10bl; Ken Akers, Great Saling 74bl, 76tr; Kindersley: Brian North / RHS Chelsea Flower Show 2010 28bc; Mark Winwood / Alpine Garden Society 79bl; Mark Winwood / Ball Colegrave 105tr; Mark Winwood / Crug Farm 72br, 73bc, 91br; Mark Winwood / Dr Mackenzie 78tr; Mark Winwood / Hampton Court Flower Show 2014 41bl; Mark Winwood / Marle Place Gardens and Gallery, Brenchley, Kent 75tr, 85br; Mark Winwood / RHS Chelsea Flower Show 2014 67bc, 103tc; Mark Winwood / RHS Malvern Flower Show 2014 71tc, 77tl, 91tr; Mark Winwood / RHS Wisley 25br, 59tr, 59br, 62tr, 64tr, 66bl, 67tr, 70tl, 70tr, 71bc, 72bl, 77tr, 77bl, 79br, 84br, 85tl, 85bl, 86br, 92br, 93br, 104tr, 108tr, 113bl, 113br, 115bl, 119br, 120tr, 120br; Peter Anderson 14br, 18tl, 20c, 33tr, 40br, 84bl, 114bl; Peter Anderson / RHS Chelsea Flower Show 2011 34cr; Peter Anderson / RHS Hampton Court Flower Show 35tr, 125tc; Peter Anderson / RHS Hampton Court Flower Show 2014 25bl; Peter Anderson / Trehane Nursery 58tr.

GAP Photos: Graham Strong 97tc.

Cover images: *Front:* **Alamy Stock Photo:** Katya Palladina / Stockimo; *Back:* **Alamy Stock Photo:** John Gollop cl; **Dorling Kindersley:** Mark Winwood / Marle Place Gardens and Gallery, Brenchley, Kent tr.

All other images © Dorling Kindersley

DK | Penguin Random House

Produced for DK by COBALT ID
www.cobaltid.co.uk

Editor Diana Vowles
Senior US Editor Megan Douglass
US Consultant John Tullock
Managing Art Editor Paul Reid
Art Editor Darren Bland

DK LONDON

Project Editor Lucy Philpott
Assistant Editor Jasmin Lennie
Senior Designer Glenda Fisher
Editorial Manager Ruth O'Rourke
Senior Production Editor Tony Phipps
Production Controller Kariss Ainsworth
Jacket Co-ordinator Emily Cannings
Art Director Maxine Pedliham
Publishing Director Katie Cowan

Jacket Designer Nicola Powling
Consultant Gardening Publisher Chris Young

First American Edition, 2024
Published in the United States by DK Publishing
1745 Broadway, 20th Floor, New York, NY 10019

Copyright © 2024 Dorling Kindersley Limited
DK, a Division of Penguin Random House LLC
24 25 26 27 28 10 9 8 7 6 5 4 3 2 1
001–338452–March/2024

A catalog record for this book
is available from the Library of Congress.
ISBN: 978-0-7440-9241-7

Printed and bound in China

www.dk.com